The
Woman's
Guide
to the
Bible

Also by Lynne Bundesen

So the Woman Went Her Way
GodDependency
Us: The People of Washington, D.C.
Dear Miss Liberty (editor)

The Woman's Guide to the Bible

Lynne Bundesen

CROSSROAD · NEW YORK

1993

The Crossroad Publishing Company
370 Lexington Avenue, New York, NY 10017

Printed in the United States of America

Library of Congress Cataloging-in-Publication Data
Bundesen, Lynne.
    The woman's guide to the Bible / by Lynne Bundesen.
      p. cm.
    Includes bibliographical references.
    ISBN 0-8245-1373-8
    1. Women in the Bible.   2. Bible — Christian, interpretation, etc.
    3. Women — Prayer-books and devotions.   I. Title.
    BS575.B84 1993.
    220.6'1'082–dc20
                                   93-28579
                                       CIP

Grateful acknowledgment is made to the Jewish Publication Society for permission to quote from *Tanakh — The Holy Scriptures: The New JPS Translation of the Holy Scriptures According to the Traditional Hebrew Text*. Used by permission.

To Hannah,
who knows who she is and where she is going,
and to Russell, who sees it

Contents

So God created man in his own image, in the image of God created
he him; male and female created he them.

(Genesis 1:27)

Thy mother is like a vine in thy blood, planted by the waters: she was
fruitful and full of branches by reason of many waters.
    And she had strong rods for the sceptres of them that bare rule,
and her stature was exalted among the thick branches, and she
appeared in her height with the multitude of her branches.
    But she was plucked up in fury, she was cast down to the ground,
and the east wind dried up her fruit: her strong rods were broken
and withered; the fire consumed them.
    And now she is planted in the wilderness, in a dry and thirsty
ground.

(Ezekiel 19:10–13)

In that day, saith the LORD, will I assemble her that halteth, and I
will gather her that is driven out, and her that I have afflicted.

(Micah 4:6)

And there appeared a great wonder in heaven; a woman clothed
with the sun, and the moon under her feet, and upon her head a
crown of twelve stars:
    And she being with child cried, travailing in birth, and pained
to be delivered.

(Revelation 12:1–2)

And to the woman were given two wings of a great eagle, that she
might fly into the wilderness, into her place, where she is nourished
for a time, and times, and half a time, from the face of the serpent.

(Revelation 12:14)

Introduction

THE BIBLE IS A NARRATIVE of spiritual power for woman. This Guide to the Bible explores that narrative of spiritual power and shows you how to explore the Bible and find that power for yourself.

Focusing on and directing our attention to the narrative of the female in the Bible, we will no longer find the textbook of our culture and our Judeo-Christian religions an obstacle to a true and familiar female spirituality.

With the Bible as our pastor, we will come to know the women of the Bible in a more intimate way. We will learn from the women of the Bible wonderful stories, inventive ways to solve problems, great lines for desperate moments, practical tips for getting our houses in order and our children in perspective. Welcomed into the homes and hearts of the women in the Bible, we will find the wisdom and authority to interpret our lives today even without a priest, rabbi or minister.

Whether we are Jews or Christians, believers or non-believers, the Bible is a non-denominational account of the spiritual self. The background of the Book that has defined politics and culture, comforted the bereft and inspired thought through the ages is, at first glance, a desert landscape dotted with camels and wells. But the foreground of the Book is consciousness — then and now, sacred and profane, male and female. Transcending a particular time, a particular culture, the Bible speaks for itself as it reveals living, detailed messages of power, strength, beauty and comfort for women today.

Just as women are at the very heart of life today, women are at the very heart of the Bible. Sometimes they have husbands, sometimes not. Sometimes they have children, sometimes not. Women travel alone, lead armies, deal with difficult, dangerous, and graceful men. Women defend their nations, interpret Holy Scripture, judge Israel, save Israel, minister to and anoint the Christ.

Sarah, Hagar, Rebekah, Rachel, Leah, Tamar, Miriam, Deborah,

1

Abigail, Ruth, Naomi, Hannah, Huldah, Esther, Mary, Mary of Magdala, Mary of Bethany, Joanna, Susanna, Priscilla, unnamed women, the powerful and powerless women of the Bible help us to recognize ourselves — our spiritual selves — and help us claim and apply that birthright in our daily lives.

Reflecting on the lives of biblical women can set us off on the most fulfilling adventure of all — the search for our spiritually created identity. For the Bible engages both intellect and emotion to answer the deepest question of all: "Who am I?"

You will notice as you look through this Guide that most chapters begin with a question. Asking yourself questions as you read the Bible will naturally sharpen your ability to think for yourself. Questions that aren't answered right away can be returned to another day, another time. The Bible has been around for a long time and you don't have to get it all in a day.

First-time readers will find this Guide a helpful overview of the Bible. While experienced readers may find that much they already know is not discussed, they will still find this Guide a companion that complements their individual or group Bible study.

Whether we are traveling alone or in a group, the Bible puts it this way: *If I take the wings of the morning, and dwell in the uttermost parts of the sea; Even there shall thy hand lead me, and thy right hand shall hold me* (Psalm 139:9–10).

Versions of the Bible

The Woman's Guide to the Bible is about the Bible as a whole; while the basic biblical text used for this Guide is The Holy Bible: King James Version, selections from other biblical translations are also used and are designated by the following abbreviations:

AT   The Bible: An American Translation

CEV   The Bible for Today's Family: Contemporary English Version

GNB   The Good News Bible

NIV   Holy Bible: New International Version

NJB   The New Jerusalem Bible

NRSV   Holy Bible: New Revised Standard Version

Phillips   The New Testament in Modern English

TNK   Tanakh — The Holy Scriptures: The New JPS Translation of the Holy Scriptures According to the Traditional Hebrew Text

Tyn   Tyndale's Old Testament

How to Begin

WHAT IF THE BIBLE WERE EASY TO READ and — in just the turn of a page — you could find the comfort, inspiration and answers you need today?

How can you read the Bible easily?

Begin by reading the Bible as the woman you are today — as the sum of all your experience.

As the woman you are today, take the Book, go into a room alone and shut the door behind you. Or, if you prefer, take the Book and go out for a walk.

This simplistic approach is deliberate. The Bible becomes more immediate if you read it alone. No one else hears with your ears, sees with your eyes, knows what you need, what you want, where you want to go in just the way that you do.

Allow yourself to be alone with the Bible and your own unlimited potential for understanding it. The Bible is a lens that magnifies your spiritual self. Reading glasses, mirrors, camera pictures and the approval of friends are poor substitutes for the vision that exists when you see the Book as a guide to your own consciousness. A Bible of your own is the passport to the greatest adventure of all — the adventure of self-realization.

The Bible you choose should be one that is yours, that speaks in language you appreciate. Choose the Bible that suits you, as you choose the music you listen to in your most private, personal moments.

Unless you read Hebrew, the original language of the Jewish Bible, or the biblical Greek language of the New Testament, you will be reading a translation. Translations of the Bible exist not only in almost every spoken language on earth but often in many styles of just one of those languages. You will probably want to compare several different translations of the Bible to find one that is easy for you to read. Some Bibles have many different translations all on the same page. This may or may not be your cup of tea.

Churches and religions use different translations of the Bible depending on their traditions. But you are not a church or religion. You are a woman about to begin reading the Bible as the woman you are today.

The Hebrew Bible of thirty-nine books is divided into three parts: the Law, the Prophets, the Writings. The New Testament has twenty-seven books. Christians who are Roman Catholics read seven additional books.

Like people, the Bible comes in all sizes and colors. The Bible is available in large type, small print, Braille, on audio tapes and all styles of computer software.

Go to a used book store, order a Bible through the mail, get one for free from a Bible society, ask a friend to buy you one, rummage through your great aunt's belongings, borrow one from the library or order one from a computer software catalogue.

Alone and comfortable, hold the Bible in your hands.

Open the Book to any page.

You are looking for inspiration, not history. The Bible does not have to be read in chronological order. Nor does this Guide.

Take two or three deep breaths.

Look down at the page and read until something catches your eye or ear. Then stop reading and remember the words that struck you or the question that was raised in your mind.

Be still for a few moments and listen quietly. Take time to reflect on the words, the images, the thoughts that arise. What you are listening for is not just the literal interpretation but the spiritual.

Make a note of the verse or words that caught your attention.

This is easy to do. Bibles have the name of the book on the top of every page. Your Bible should include a table of contents, indicating the page on which each book begins. Chapters are numbered, as are verses. When you read, for example, Genesis 1:1, you know you are in the Book of Genesis, first chapter, first verse. All Bibles use the same chapter and verse markings.

The chapter and verse of references used in this Guide are noted. Don't feel that you necessarily have to look up each and every reference any more than you would have to visit each and every town on a map. But, as on a map, at least you know where places are located in the overall scheme of the territory. And should you want to visit particular places, you know where to go and how to get there. Before you have traveled far at all in the Guide you will know how to find for yourself anything or any place in your Bible.

There are wonderful promises, lyric passages, profound parables and endless common sense throughout the pages of the Original Text. The Bible is broad and deep, and comfort lies within its pages. If you open to a classic, the Twenty-third Psalm, for instance, and find yourself by the familiar *still waters,* fine. But there are also horror stories, genealogies (the "begats" some people call them) and seemingly tedious and detailed instructions on how to build a tabernacle or test a wife for faithfulness.

If you should open your Book to a less-than-pleasant place, do not be dismayed. There are tough times and great times in any and every life. And the Bible points them out — rough places as well as the plain.

Mark the date next to the phrase or word that caught your attention. Write in your Bible if you want to do so. Keep a separate notebook if that appeals to you. This is your process of discovery.

Be honest. If you have a hostile reaction, write that down. If you think you merely like the sound of a phrase, write that down. If you need the Bible only for a moment's comfort, don't close the Book before you make a note of the place where that comfort was found.

Be wise. Make notes of your own observations. Cherish them. But don't necessarily share your first discoveries with friends, family or church. The process of reading the Bible is about you — where you are and where you are going. Like your own life, the Bible relates to itself. Patterns appear and develop as you look at more than one part of your life. Patterns appear in the Bible as you look at more than one line, one phrase.

You don't need a degree in theology in order to appreciate what the Bible is saying. But you do need a Bible concordance. A concordance is an alphabetical index to biblical words with a reference to the sentence in which each word appears and usually some part of the context. Computer concordances are also available.

The paperback compact edition of *Strong's Exhaustive Concordance of the Bible* — the easiest to handle and most thorough concordance to the King James Version of the Bible — shows every word of that translation of the Bible in alphabetical order. Each word is assigned a number for cross-reference to the original Hebrew or Greek. Strong's numbering system is used by most other biblical references that use original language.

The *NIV* (New International Version) *Exhaustive Concordance* for that version of the Bible adds an additional numbering system developed by a computer concordance team.

Cruden's is a nice and easy-to-use concordance. And many versions of the Bible contain concordances as well as maps, alternate readings, the words of Jesus in red, dictionaries, chain-references and textual footnotes.

Using a concordance not only tells you where to find words in the Bible but can totally transform your understanding of the Book. As the Bible often speaks in allegory, simile and parable, a concordance easily takes you into those dimensions of thought.

Take, for example, the word *Lebanon*. Most know it as a once-peaceful, then war-torn country still now in difficult circumstances. *Strong's Concordance* shows that the word *Lebanon* appears 71 times in the King James Version and assigns *Lebanon* the number 3844. Turning to number 3844 in *Strong's,* you will see that the word *Lebanon* is from the Hebrew root *heart* (the most interior organ) and defines *Lebanon* as "white mountain" (from its snow). Some of the biblical references to *Lebanon* may be merely geographical. But others connote much more.

> *Is it not yet a very little while, and* Lebanon *shall be turned into a fruitful field, and the fruitful field shall be esteemed as a forest?* (Isaiah 29:17)

If the word *Lebanon* here is read as meaning your "heart," the verse takes on a new, richer meaning. Read it again and substitute *my heart* for *Lebanon*. Savor the promise.

> *Is it not yet a very little while, and* my heart *shall be turned into a fruitful field, and the fruitful field shall be esteemed as a forest?*

Any word in the Bible can be looked up in the same way. Should you want to know how to be a better mother, how to get along with your own mother or what being a mother might mean to your spiritual as well as biological life, then you will want to fulfill that desire and start by looking up in your Bible the word *mother.*

You will find 244 references to *mother* — the first in Genesis 2:24. You will also find 75 references to *mother's,* 7 to *mothers* and only 1 to *Mother* with a capital *M.* You will find, further, that there are different kinds of mothers, different thoughts about mothers, seeming paradoxes and contradictions about mothers. You will still find a verse or a thought that applies to your own question or situation.

Even the "begats" can take on new meaning if we use a concordance. The first genealogy listed in the Bible is in the fifth chapter of Genesis — the genealogy of Adam, Seth, Enos, Cainan, Mahaleel, Jared, Enoch, Methusaleh, Lamech, Noah. This genealogy conveys more than one message.

If you read the list literally, skim over it or dismiss it as an example demonstrating that the Bible is about men long dead, you will miss the message. With a little digging, what on the surface looks like a boring chronological history of generations becomes, instead, a message of spiritual promise and hope.

A translation in one interpretation of the Hebrew meaning of those names suggests Man (Adam), Placed (Seth), Incurable Sickness (Enos), Deplorable (Cainan), The Blessed God (Mahaleel), Descends (Jared), Teaching (Enoch), Death Sent Away (Methusaleh), to the Distressed (Lamech), Comfort/Rest (Noah).

Read as narrative it says that man placed in incurable sickness is deplorable, and therefore the Blessed God descends, teaching that death be sent away and bringing to the distressed comfort and rest.

This may seem a stretch at first glance. But it seems less so if you are familiar with a concordance, those names in Hebrew, with the variety of their implications and interpretations and with the fact that the Bible's message is not about patriarchy but about God's Word speaking to your daily life.

Millions upon hundreds of millions today turn to the Bible. Some do so in an irksome self-righteousness, others from terror, others more for hope, for guidance in the complexities of the world.

You have turned in quiet to the Bible for some glimpses of what it might hold for you.

You have chosen a Bible that suits you, reached into a verse or text, an easy or hard place, listened, watched, made a note, kept it to yourself. Now, how to begin a fuller journey into the pages of the Bible and your spiritual life?

Without anyone looking over your shoulder, to catch sight of the Bible as a whole turn to the beginning, to Genesis and the opening words of the Book.

In the beginning God created the heaven and the earth.

(Genesis 1:1)

Your journey is under way.

Chapter One

In the Beginning

WHAT IF THE BIBLICAL GOD IS NOT A MAN?

What if the biblical Creator is Spirit?

Genesis 1:1 to 2:3 describes the Creation of the universe by an all-good, all-powerful God. The Creation — not just of all objects, but of all ideas — sets the tone for the entire Bible. All else, all the remainder of the pages that comprise the texts of the Hebrew and Christian holy words are commentaries. Backgrounds and foregrounds, highlights and dim places, all politics, history, art, relations between men and women, all stand in relation to Genesis 1.

Let's look at what the opening lines of the Bible say about the Creator.

> *In the beginning God created the heaven and the earth. And the earth was without form, and void; and darkness was upon the face of the deep. And the Spirit of God moved upon the face of the waters.* (Genesis 1:1–2)

Spirit of God, in the original Hebrew, is *ruach Elohiym. Ruach,* the word meaning "Spirit," is a feminine noun. *Elohiym* is the plural form of God. Nothing is said about a bearded old man in flowing white robes.

What is said is that Spirit, denoted by a feminine, plural word, is Creator and moves.

As you read the Bible never forget that all life springs from Spirit.

There is no fearsome Father to run from, no overbearing Mother, no absent Parent to search for.

Remind yourself, make a note if you need to, no matter what you might have heard before, the Creator is not a large man. This reminder will help demystify the Bible for you and reveal recurring views of the God of the Bible as Spirit, Life.

11

The ideas outlined in the early verses of Genesis may seem simple to you, or they may take you some time to absorb. What the Bible says in its first verses may seem either literal or abstract so that you may just want to skim the surface and turn to stories of women and men found later in the Bible and this Guide.

But even if you don't begin at the beginning you will want to return to the ideas expressed in those verses, because the deeper meanings of biblical stories are found there. A plunge into the treasure-laden depths of the spiritual Creation described from Genesis 1:1 to Genesis 2:3 can be exhilarating.

You will want to read this Creation account for yourself. For now let's slip under the face of biblical waters, look into the well of Scripture and its overarching themes and see just a smattering of the bounty that lies beneath the surface of a few key words in the first chapter of the Bible.

In the beginning

If you've ever dipped into biblical waters, you will already have recognized that in the Bible things happen in two different kinds of time. The opening of the Bible describes one kind of time — *in the beginning*. This kind of time is spiritual time, or synchronous, simultaneous coexistence — everything good that ever was or will be happening present in this moment. We hint at this biblical kind of time when we speak of immortality, eternal life, born again and never dying, when we say "forever."

Simultaneous time can't be measured or budgeted by a clock or by the lowering and rising of sun or tides. It's not variable. The message of synchronous time is spiritual, perfect unvarying love. Not, "I loved you on July 31, but not on August 9." Not, "I loved you when you wore that little black dress but not when you were in your green slacks."

The second kind of time can be measured by the clock and by genealogies. It's historical and chronological — the "my mother was born in ..." kind of time or, "I'll meet you at eight o'clock" kind of time.

The distinction is important. Among other things the distinction explains miracles. The time referred to as in the beginning describes Spirit, God extending, appearing, acting throughout the cosmos simultaneously. This kind of time is freedom, endless bliss, perfect peace, continuing spiritual and scientific exploration. This kind of time can reach you wherever you are in chronological or "clock" time.

What we call miracles are intersections of the two kinds of time — examples of timeless truth meeting the lives of women and men in clock time.

Further, wholly spiritual biblical time holds only joy. No sorrow. In chronological time there is joy but also sorrow. Reason enough to turn away from the clock and look deeply into spiritual Creation. Then, as you look at the miracles in the Bible — or the miracles in your life — you might well see what is going on as the light, revelation, the ideas of spiritual Creation that illumine historical time.

Water

Water plays such an important role in the Bible that one cannot possibly consider only its literal meaning. As we have read in Genesis 1:2, *the Spirit of God moved on the face of the waters*. In the "big ticket" events of the early chapters of the Bible — Noah, the Ark and the Flood; the parting of the sea where Miriam, Moses and Aaron and the other women and men of Israel escape from Egypt — *water* is a metaphor for and the physical manifestation of the first element of Creation. In the baptisms described still later in the Bible (Matthew 3:11), there is *water*. And Jesus walks on *water*, and he changes *water* into wine.

For just a hint of how central *water* is to biblical messages, look in your concordance for the place to find Rachel and Jacob at the well; look up the *woman of Samaria* who, after recognizing the Christ, leaves her waterpot; find the pure *river* of *water* of life. It's no exaggeration to say that one could spend a lifetime of profitable study of biblical *water* — seas, oceans, rivers, rain, snow, hail, dew and the mixture of *water* and light, the rainbow.

Think of *water* as Spirit's Presence every time it rains, every time you see or walk in the snow, every time you are by a river, at the swimming pool, as you are washing the clothes or the dishes, taking a shower or bath, every time tears well up in your eyes or stream down your face. You'll be surprised at how often *water* can remind you of spiritual Creation.

And God said

The same process that describes Spirit moving on the face of the *waters* includes *and God said*. One translation from the Hebrew makes this first activity of moving and the Word of *Elohiym* one event. In that Hebrew translation we are still in the first sentence of Scripture with the uttering of the Word.

The revelation of spiritual Creation comes into focus with the words, *And God said*.

And the first thing God says is:

Let there be light: and there was light. (Genesis 1:3)

Light

When we say that we "see the light" on a topic or idea, we are referring to seeing the truth of something. And in Genesis the original Hebrew word *light* is *or,* often referred to, or translated as, "revelation" and/or "truth." We will follow *light* throughout the Bible.

All Creation in the first chapter of Genesis takes place in the *light*. Though there is yet no sun, moon or stars, still there is *light*. Biblical Creation is revealed; more specifically, the truth of what already exists is revealed.

Look at it this way.

Picture yourself moving through a darkened house.

Say that you were there when the plans were drawn and you know them by heart, know the whole house is perfect in every detail from the foundation to the view. Without light you can think of what is in the house. Things can be felt though nothing can be seen.

At hand is a light switch. Touch it and the room in which you stand floods with light. In stages your eye takes in every inch, every nook and cranny, everything that has been purposefully, carefully, artfully placed in the room for nourishment, comfort and rest.

In a way that's how Genesis 1:3 describes Creation. Everything is there, but the *light* makes it visible.

From Spirit moving on the *waters* to God's Word to *Light,* the process of Spirit's activity is unbroken.

And the Word names, and naming brings into Being.

God's Words define and make distinction. There is one Source, but not one big blur. So, in the first chapter of Genesis, light is day and not night. And, as we read, we see what we now take for granted: morning is not evening, dry land is not water, fruit trees are not grass, the moon is not the sun, birds are not whales. Each and every idea is distinct, individual, and moves in the context of *Elohiym*.

It is in the *light* that all good can be seen, and there is no question of the biblical significance of *light*.

Revelation, the last book of the Bible, graphically depicts *light* and darkness. Track the *light* all the way to the end of the Bible to see the spiritual signification described in this first chapter of the Book.

Third day

The *third day* of Creation is pregnant with activity and meaning (Genesis 1:9–13). References to the *third day* appear throughout the Bible. As you stay alert to *the third day* you will see when that day is mentioned, stories move into another dimension. On the biblical *third day* look for the change between the historical story and the spiritual presentation.

The biblical *third day* includes not only the gathering of the *waters* into seas but the appearance of the earth. Let's take a look here, in the midst of the third day, at just one well-known Bible story.

The story of Miriam, Moses and Aaron and the women, men and children of Israel going through the Sea is an example of how the Bible puts the words and ideas of just the first ten verses of the first chapter of Genesis into action.

In the familiar account of Moses parting the Sea, *in the beginning* time meets "clock" time just as the Egyptians are about to overtake the children of Israel (Exodus 14:21). The *water* parts because, as we have read in the first verse of Genesis, Spirit has already moved on the face of the *waters,* and in the ninth verse of Genesis — describing the third day — the *waters* are gathered together. *And God said, "Let the waters under the sky be gathered in one place, and let dry ground appear." And it was so. God called the dry ground "land," and the gathered waters he called "seas." And God saw that it was good* (Genesis 9–10 *NIV*).

The *waters* are already divided. *In the beginning* time has met "clock" time. The lives of the children of Israel are spared. Timeless truth has met the need of the day. The parting of the *waters* is not a miracle in the abstract sense, nor merely a one-time intervention.

The parting of the *waters* is the work of spiritual Creation. The dry land appears. And just in time.

There is so much about the activity of the third day throughout the Bible that it's worth special attention.

> *And God said, "Let the earth sprout vegetation: seed-bearing plants and fruit trees of every kind on earth that bear fruit with the seed in it." And it was so. The earth brought forth vegetation, seed-bearing plants of every kind, and trees of every kind bearing fruit with the seed in it. And God saw that this was good. And there was evening and there was morning, a third day.* (Genesis 1:11–13 *TNK*)

The *seed is in itself,* says the King James Version (Genesis 1:11). When we plant an acorn, the oak tree that will arise from the acorn is already within. Every plant and tree, every thing and every idea are already made, but we would need the lens of simultaneous time to see through chronological time in order to see everything already made.

But there is to be something particularly essential for women to understand about the *seed within itself.* At this point in Genesis there is no division of male and female. But later, after gender and sex are introduced into biblical accounts, we will see that there are to be attacks on the seed of woman. We will want to return to this verse in Genesis more than a few times as it is the spiritual reality, or Spirit, against which these attacks are directed.

Once more. A look at two kinds of time — illustrated by the creative activity and symbolism of *the third day* — is essential for an appreciation of key events in the Bible. As you familiarize yourself with the spiritual implications in *the third day,* you may notice your own experience makes its way safely through conflicted, turbulent or difficult waters and takes on another dimension with less confinement.

Fourth

Fourth is another word in the feminine gender (Hebrew), and on the fourth day God says, *Let there be two great lights* (Genesis 1:14–19). These *lights divide* the day from the night, as the firmament of verse 6 *divides* the *waters* from the *waters.* The *lights* are set in the *firmament of heaven to give light upon the earth and to rule over the day and over the night, and to divide the light from the darkness.*

If these two *great lights* are to mean the sun and the moon, then their emergence takes place in a feminine context. The *lights* appear as *signs and for seasons, and for days, and years* and, at one simple level, can be taken to be a possible reason women feel particularly connected to the marking of days and years as important elements of life.

The reader will want to further note the use of the words *rule over.* The issue of "ruling" is found in the Bible — as in life today — touching political, social and marital relations. The Bible uses the word *rule* in both a literal and prophetic sense. Here the word *rule* is used in a female context and performs the essential function of dividing *light* from darkness.

Abundantly

> *And God said, Let the waters bring forth abundantly the moving creature that hath life, and fowl that may fly above the earth in the open firmament of heaven.* (Genesis 1:20)

So too with the whales and other living creatures. The *waters* bring them forth *abundantly,* and of the revelation of this fifth day — like the revelation of the third and fourth — it says that *God saw that it was good* (Genesis 1:12, 18, 21).

This idea of abundance has real import for the preservation of all species. Spiritual Creation elucidated in the first chapter of Genesis is the launching point for religious concern about the environment.

The use of the word *abundantly* as a reference to the first chapter of Genesis takes on added biblical significance and poignancy when Moses strikes a rock and the *water came out abundantly* and all the congregation and their beasts drank (Numbers 20:11), when in Psalm 132:15 it says, *I will abundantly bless her provision,* and when Jesus says, *I am come that they might have life, and that they might have it more abundantly* (John 10:10).

No virtue is necessarily gained nor points awarded for starvation, physical or emotional. The biblical Creator, the Spirit of the first chapter of Genesis, provides abundantly.

Female image

*And God said, Let us make man in our image, after our like-
ness: and let them have dominion over the fish of the sea, and
over the fowl of the air, and over the cattle, and over all the
earth, and over every creeping thing that creepeth upon the
earth. So God created man in his own image, in the image
of God created he him; male and female created he them.*
(Genesis 1:26–27)

In this ascendent order of Creation, from *light* to Day and Night,
to Heaven and Earth to Seas and land to plant to fish to fowl to beast,
to male and female, the female is the last. Not the least but the last —
as the last note or chord of a symphony represents the completion
and fulfillment of the entire musical piece. The *man* created is the
reflective of the plural *Elohiym* in the first verses — *male and female.* Whether you read *male and female* to mean two separate
genders or one *image,* including both genders as a compound idea,
the female that you are is the highest idea in the revelation of Spirit's
unfolding Creation.

Blessed

And then the crowning achievement, a seventh or Sabbath day of
rest in which to survey, set a stamp on and reflect on the whole of
Creation. Just as the living creatures of the fifth day and the *male and
female* of the sixth day are *blessed* (Genesis 1:22, 28), so too is this
rest of the seventh day *blessed* (Genesis 2:3).

There are countless examples of good and blessing throughout
the Bible, but you already know by now that when examples such
as *water,* the *third day,* the *seed within itself* appear, they are re-
minders that the story is not merely historical but points to unlimited
good — spiritual territory.

If you want to explore and settle in spiritual territory, you will find
biblical texts that describe the *light* and the path to that land and its
capital, the holy city. The holy city detailed at the end of the Bible
in the Book of Revelation 21:2 describes a full-circle return to the
glories of your completely ordered, fully endowed spiritual identity
of the spiritual Creation presented by Genesis 1:1–2:3.

But on that path you will pass by the Garden of Eden, where
gullible, victimized, incomplete women and weak, frightened, jeal-

ous dust-men pass the days of their lives young and restless, old and forlorn. Let's drop in on the First Couple and the original soap opera. When we see what their lives (and the lives of their children) are like, we may wonder why anyone would want Adam and Eve in their family tree.

Chapter Two

The Seed and the Serpent

HAVE YOU EVER FELT as if you don't have your own distinct identity? That you exist only in relation to a man?

Have you ever felt you are walking around in a dream? Do you ever feel that everything you do comes out wrong? That as a woman you are being blamed for things that are not your fault?

Welcome to the wonderful world of Eve.

But what if the story of Adam and Eve in the Garden of Eden is neither simply ancient myth nor a divine mandate to suffer for sin? What if it's a classic description of contemporary consciousness, reflecting relations between men and women on earth today?

You don't have to be a feminist or a rocket scientist to be aware that Eve's story reflects thousands of years of almost exclusively male interpretation of Bible texts.

And when only men interpreted the Bible, reports filtered down to the general population that a woman, Eve, was the root cause of all sin, sickness and death. Some reports today say that even now woman must atone for Eve's sin.

Poor woman.

Poor Eve.

She wakes up next to a man she does not know. Before long she has doomed all humanity. That's what a literal out-of-context reading of the Adam and Eve story might lead you to believe — if it stood alone. But it doesn't. Eve's story stands in relation to spiritual Creation and woman's already revealed timeless identity as image of Spirit, God.

Let's take a fresh look into this classic tale to see if, in fact, it says Eve, woman, is responsible for everything terrible that ever happened. Let's see what the story might have to tell us about recognizing and disentangling some of the problems you encounter as the woman you are today.

Through the mist

After the first account of Creation is laid out, the Bible presents another creation, introducing the concept of evil. From then on, side by side, lie the unhappy parts of the Bible, the parts where innocents are slaughtered and cities laid waste, and the happy parts, where lives are long and full and cities and nations built up. Sometimes the two accounts of Creation are mixed together within a sentence, verse or story. Recognizing these places may not come in a moment. But the first glimpse of a text that carries more than one message can be breathtaking.

As you read for yourself you will see that in the evil parts there is a mist, a denseness, darkness, despair, destruction, dishonor, domination, death — all the things and more that you have heard the Bible is about.

But there is cause for hope. In the good parts, it is as if the mist dissolves and glimpses of the first account of Creation are clear. When the mist thins you can see the spiritual. Through the thinned mist, in the good parts there is *light,* dignity, healing and self-respect, those things not associated with Adam or Eve or the punishing God of their creation.

The story of Adam and Eve is not the story of spiritual Creation. The story of Adam and Eve is not really even a continuation of the first account of Creation. It is a second and entirely different story of Creation, but it is set against the backdrop of that revelation where the *Spirit* (female) of *Elohiym* (plural, God) is visible in a *light*-filled spiritual and complete universe. In fact, the story of creation in the Garden is nothing compared to the first account of Creation.

Our introduction to the Garden of Eden (Genesis 2:4–3:24) goes like this: Instead of *Spirit* moving on the *waters* and the Word introducing light, a mist comes up from the earth and covers everything.

Instead of a *blessed male and female* emerging as the penultimate achievement of *Elohiym* the Creator, a God with a different

name (the *Lord God*) makes first a man out of the dust of the ground
and breathes life into him through his nose. The Hebrew word for
dust is *adamah,* from which comes the name Adam.

This Lord God makes a garden and puts the dust-man into it. This
garden is called Eden. The root of this word is *pleasure.*

Lord God also puts some trees in the garden. One, in the *midst,* is
the tree of life. The other, in no specific location, is a tree of both *good
and evil.* That there is no specific location given to the knowledge of
good and evil is significant. The Bible is describing a scene in which
life is clearly marked and placed. What is not life has no place and
no specificity.

A *river* comes out of the garden and separates into four rivers.
Rivers have special biblical signification for women, and we will see
rivers again and again, into the final book of the Bible, Revelation.

The Lord God takes the man and puts him in the garden again,
although there is no mention that he has ever left it.

Good *and* evil

And Lord God tells the man to eat from any tree but the tree of *the
knowledge of good and evil.* The warning is that if the man eats of *the
knowledge of good and evil he shall surely die.* Knowing evil as well
as good causes death. The Bible repeats this idea over and over and
reminds us to know only *good.* And the reader has probably noted
that this is the first biblical mention of evil and of death.

The Lord God says it's *not good* to have man alone. *Good,* we
know, is *male and female* created simultaneously and not one at
a time. This creation of Adam alone is already *not good.* In further
reversal of spiritual Creation, when this Lord God then makes beasts
and fowls, the man, instead of God, names them. But still, for Adam,
there is no *help meet,* no helper (Genesis 2:18).

So the Lord God puts Adam into a *deep sleep,* and while Adam is
in this coma God takes a rib out of him and makes a *woman.*

The Lord God presents the surgically created woman to Adam.
Adam claims her as his own flesh, and — as the tradition that would
follow has had a woman take the man's name at marriage — Adam
names her after part of himself. Adam calls her *Woman because she
was taken out of Man* (Genesis 2:23).

And it is for this cause, the Bible says, that a man *shall leave his
father and his mother, and shall cleave unto his wife: and they shall*

be one flesh. And they were both naked, the man and his wife, and were not ashamed (Genesis 2:24–25).

We will see the first part of this phrase again in the Book of Ephesians, chapter 5, verse 31, where it rests in an entirely other context.

But continuing for now in Eden, it is at this point (Genesis 3:1) that something happens that we will see again and again in the Bible. The story that started with a man moves to a woman and her situation or condition. It moves, as we shall see, to where the action is going to take place.

A talking serpent appears out of nowhere and asks the woman, *"Did God really say, 'You must not eat from any tree in the garden'?"* (Genesis 3:1 *NIV*)

An element of doubt has been introduced.

The woman says God told them they will die if they eat that fruit from the tree in the midst of the garden.

The talking serpent trivializes while telling the woman that she is wrong, that she has been sold a bill of goods.

Tush ye shall not die, the serpent says (Genesis 3:4 *Tyn*) as if to say, never mind, it's *nothing*. No big deal. The talking serpent suggests to the woman that a *knowledge* of both *evil and good* will change and improve her situation. All the woman has to do — the suggestion says — is to eat a fruit that looks good and makes *one wise* and then she will be like God (or gods, depending on the translation) and know *good and evil.* (We know that God — the Spirit of Creation in the first chapter of Genesis — knows only *good.*)

Trivialized and seduced to death, the woman eats. She gives some to her husband. He eats (Genesis 3:6).

As you read these first six verses of the second chapter of Genesis for yourself, you will see what happens next. Things do change. But not for the better. The woman is tricked. Now she is not *wise* but *ashamed.* This introduction of shame into the story can be viewed as a falling from the knowledge of only good. It can also be viewed as a consequence of holding two conflicting ideas in conscious thought at the same time.

If you want to avoid the woman's dilemma and don't want to fall victim to doubt and seduction, if you want to be wise and find wisdom, this is a fine place to use your concordance.

Searching through the Scriptures for *wise* women and feminine *wisdom* you will find reference after reference.

Looking at the entire Book of Proverbs in the light of the use of *wise* and *wisdom,* you will see that much of Proverbs is not merely age-old good advice but commentary on woman — who she is and how the world receives her work. You will see also how the Bible refers to, elaborates on and repeats ideas that have been introduced in the first few chapters of Genesis.

Look especially at Proverbs 1:20–21; 3:5–6; 7:4–5; 9:8–9; 14:1; and 31:10–31.

On a day-to-day basis it's fairly hard to avoid subtle suggestions that may later make you feel foolish and ashamed; nevertheless a knowledge of what wisdom is and what wise women act like can really reduce the occasions you might be misled.

The first blame

Adam, . . . where art thou? asks the Lord God (Genesis 3:9). Adam says that he was hiding from God. Lord God asks if Adam has eaten the fruit. Just a question.

The man answers, *the woman whom thou gavest to be with me, she gave me of the tree and I did eat* (Genesis 3:12).

Where the man points the responsibility to Lord God and then to the woman and then himself, the woman sticks to reporting the facts.

The difference in their responses reflects much of the same conflict that exists between men and women throughout history and today. Many women today who might feel that men hide when a problem or a potential problem arises can look at the Adam story again. Many who feel that men are particularly defensive and do not immediately assume responsibility for a mistake can see from the story that when the blame is pointed it is often pointed elsewhere and often to the woman.

If you find yourself in a place where avoidance, blame of woman and male abdication of direct responsibility are in the air, you might well recognize that you are not in spiritual territory but in the shame-filled atmosphere of Eden. You don't have to stay there.

Reminding yourself that you are the product of the spiritual Creation will not make you arrogant nor turn you into a person who denies reality. Nor will it separate you from God. It will, however, give you the spiritual, mental, emotional and moral resources necessary to see your way out of victimization.

Claiming your heritage as the female of the first account of Creation may give you the exact thing to say, the move to make or place to go that will separate you from the notion that you are somehow Eve or related to her.

The woman answers

"What is this you have done?" (Genesis 3:13 *NIV*) the Lord God asks the woman. She does not hide nor does she elaborate nor does she lie. She answers directly: *"The serpent deceived me, and I ate"* (Genesis 3:13 *NIV*).

The Lord God curses the serpent and puts hatred between the serpent and the woman and between the *seed* of the serpent and *the seed* of the woman (Genesis 3:15).

Here is the introduction of a theme we see throughout the Bible and throughout life today. Evidence of the hatred of woman and her *seed* in today's world can be found in homes, nations, streets, the workplace and the courts. There seems to be a very, very long way to go before the end of the conflict.

But rather than suffer through the ages it takes to end the conflict, let's look ahead here and turn to the first verse in chapter 12 of the Book of Revelation. In this chapter the magnitude of the conflict between the seed of the woman and the seed of the serpent is clear. The proportions have changed dramatically, but this story in Revelation is the story in the Garden of Eden writ large.

To say that the woman has grown is an understatement. No longer Eve, helpless and confused, this biblical woman *is clothed with the sun, and the moon under her feet, and upon her head a crown of twelve stars* (Revelation 12:1).

The woman is *travailing* (Revelation 12:2). All her being is working to give birth, to deliver, to bring forth new life. The serpent has grown into a *great red dragon* (Revelation 12:3). And the woman is protected in the *wilderness, where she has a place prepared of God* (Revelation 12:6 *NRSV*) and the *earth helped the woman* (Revelation 12:16).

There may be wilderness experiences but the Bible promises that God and the earth will help (not harm) the woman in travail and under attack. As you take a breath at this point, you may want to ponder the imagery of the sun, moon and stars, remembering the *fourth day.*

You will see as you read on in this chapter of Revelation that the woman *brought forth a man child who was to rule all nations with a rod of iron: and her child was caught up unto God and to his throne* (Revelation 12:5). The attack fails in its purpose.

The struggle of woman and her offspring saved from hatred threads through the Scriptures. The Books of Psalms, Isaiah, Jeremiah, Micah, John and 1 Thessalonians speak of the woman in travail. And there are many stories of women and children protected from evil.

When we remember the Bible is about consciousness, this theme and the struggle of woman described in the Bible go a long way toward explaining why — as you try today to bring children and ideas to fulfillment on earth — you might feel threatened and attacked. But the Bible says you will receive help. You can expect help.

Look further to Revelation 21:2 and you will see another image associated with woman — this time as *bride.* That is where the Bible is headed. As you read the Bible, don't be appalled or stand aghast that from Eve on, woman will be under attack. She, you, woman, women are also protected and elevated to the spiritual status of Genesis 1:26–27 and Revelation 22:17.

The attack may be described literally as on *woman* and her *seed,* but essentially the attacks are on the *seed within itself* described on the third day in the first chapter of Genesis. Hard as it may be to see when you are under attack, the Bible indicates that such attacks are as much against Spirit — against the idea of timeless self-completeness — as against you personally.

To say that much happens to and for women before the final drama that begins in Eden is an understatement. Women in the Bible deal with hatred. They face up to hatred, succumb to it, avoid it, master it, watch it dissolve and disappear. Most biblical women dwell, not just in tents but, metaphorically, in the consciousness of their spiritual rights. Like women today, biblical women illustrate the activity of *good* in human life. And the good news of Revelation is that the woman and her seed are saved. The overblown serpent is cast out of consciousness forever.

It shouldn't be difficult for you to see your own experience as swinging back and forth somewhere between Genesis and Revelation, between Eve and the bride. The ebbing and flowing of doubts, temptations, mistakes, and protections when there is trouble make a lot more sense when you see that the Bible explains this process as part of the story of your life; it's not just conflict after conflict, with no way out.

Now you have seen the first and the last of the Bible.

All the day-to-day of life is in between that beginning and that ending.

Bodily consequences

See, as you read your Bible, if, in fact, it says that the descendants of Eve are to be cursed. Eve is to have *sorrow in childbirth* (Genesis 3:16), but are you?

There is much territory that remains to be explored on the subject of how *Eve* affects women's bodies today. Women's bodies, some say because of Eve and others say because of a lack of attention and understanding, have become the playground for a host of opinions and ills. Many generations of women have referred to their monthly menstrual cycles as the *curse*. This *curse* on Eve has somehow filtered down to the consciousness of women today.

Investigations into different standards of medical treatment for women and men reflect layers and layers of Adam-like assumptions. The assumption has been that with the key exception of sexual organs, women's and men's bodies are the same. Assuming a man's body to be the standard for all bodies has resulted in research that draws conclusions based solely on men, with repercussions in every area of women's health.

The chasm of negative consequences that result from the Eve story are only now being probed. We can't forget that the Eve story tells us that her body is not fully her own possession. What would a woman's body be if it had always been thought of as having been created directly by Spirit and not out of the rib of a dust-man? What if a woman's body is meant to be a reflection of Spirit and uniquely her own possession in that Spirit?

Use your concordance and do some research on body, the parts of the body and allusions to body, to soul, to sense (sensation). Perspective on the story of Adam and Eve will lessen the tension you may feel and may well help you appreciate your own body.

Sexual politics

Moreover, with regard to the curses placed on Adam, Eve and the serpent, the text says *your desire shall be for your husband, and he shall rule over you* (Genesis 3:16 *NRSV*).

Reading this specific text — in context — we remember that this *rule over* happens not in the *light* of spiritual Creation but in a mist. And, as we have already read that *male and female* are made by God simultaneously, equal as notes of the musical scale are equal, to say that one note *rules over* another note is obviously absurd.

Then what are we to make of the phrase *rule over?* We recognize the phrase from the fourth day of spiritual Creation. There the two *great lights* are set in the *firmament of the heaven to give light upon the earth, and to* rule over *the day and over the night, and to divide the light from the darkness* (Genesis 1:16–18). In Eden, the phrase relates to the woman whose body has come out of her husband's. One pictures the portrayals of her as cowering before God.

But contrast this with the picture of woman in Revelation. There one sees that the woman is standing on top of one of the *great lights*. The moon is *under her feet*. And she is *clothed with the sun* (Revelation 12:1). One might say that the woman has the proper sense of *ruling over* under control.

Reminding us more of Eden than Revelation, much of the conflict between women and men today is over who controls a woman's body.

And whereas it's obvious that the lights in the sky are not despotic rulers over day and night, sometimes it's not so obvious in relations between wives and husbands. Whereas it is obvious that the sun and moon are simply there and unaware of just who is basking in their light, too often there is a struggle between men and women over who is doing what and who benefits and how much. Sometimes the moon and sun are resplendent, breathtaking, but still they function according to a principle. The principle of male and female has been laid out in the first chapter of Genesis and is further elaborated upon throughout the Bible in a variety of places and situations.

But even in the myth of separation and fragmentation there is a hint of the oneness of male and female. It is as if even the most convoluted of notions still hints that male and female are one. There is much more to be contemplated even in the inverted use of *rule over.* The experienced Bible reader — whether or not she has a husband — has probably already used her concordance to research the 120 references to *husband*, and she has looked deeply into the relationship between desire and prayer.

Any reader will feel more at peace with the Scriptures as she looks at Isaiah 54:5 and reads, *For your Maker is your husband*. No reader can afford to miss Psalm 136 and Jeremiah 31:31–33 for more insight into who made you and who is your husband and what it means to the sense of direction you are to experience in your daily life."

Although it will take some historical time and much *travail*, at the end of the Bible, *rule over* will melt into a union of masculine and feminine qualities — a return to the image of the first account of Creation.

If, as a woman, you are feeling manipulated by the concept of *ruled over*, you will want to return to the first chapter of Genesis, where you are the daughter of Creation. Reflecting on, dwelling in spiritual Creation, where you are the highest, not a fragmentary, idea, puts things back in order and restores your spiritual rights. You will understand who you truly are and who controls what you do, where you go and what you are doing here today.

In the meantime, men who congratulate themselves on some fancied God-given right to dominate may want to leave the Garden of Eden at this point because the story goes on:

> *And unto the man he said, "Because you have listened to the voice of your wife, and have eaten of the tree about which I commanded you, 'You shall not eat of it,' cursed is the ground because of you; in toil you shall eat of it all the days of your life."* (Genesis 3:17 *NRSV*)

This verse, too, has left a legacy. Men who find it painful to listen to women's voices (or instructions) may be hanging on to the notion that they, like Adam, are cursed because they listened to their wives. Accepting the guilt of Adam is hard work and not profitable. We will see further in the Bible that God directs men to listen to women to the advantage of the whole of humanity as well as to themselves.

The biblical men who do listen to women are the ones whose names we remember today. Abraham, Isaac, Jacob and Paul listen to women and act on what the women say. Women tell David and Jesus what to do and these men listen to them. You will find some relevant examples in Genesis 16:2; 21:12; 27:43; and Mark 7:28–29.

Readers will find that many biblical women claim their God-given spiritual, moral and legal rights. When we become more nearly acquainted with biblical women, it won't be difficult to appreciate that women today, regardless of denomination or religious belief, are often following their example.

Interpreting the story of Eve as God's curse on today's women can overwhelm one with guilt, shame and domination.

On the other hand there is no reason to leap to the conclusion that the story of Adam and Eve reflects Divine Order. Certainly the account may be seen to reflect God's care and concern by showing us the contrast between what spiritual life really is and what it is not. Spiritual life is not hindered by ambiguity.

Others, of course, read the account of Eden to say that the consequence of ambiguity is suffering.

What you think about Creation

Let's reflect a minute on the Creation accounts so far. Separating one account from the other is essential to making sense of biblical stories and messages.

Dismissing the narrative of Adam and Eve as "merely" myth is difficult for many reasons. It's impossible to dismiss any part of the Bible if you believe that the Book is the inspired word of God. And so much of life seems equally as convoluted as the drama in the garden, even though man is no longer made out of dust nor woman from rib; the roots of this myth run very deep.

Dismissing the first account of Creation is even more difficult. How else to account for good? The first chapter of Genesis tells us about a spiritual God who creates and sees this Creation as *good.*

The second chapter of Genesis relates a story in which God has a different name, the Deity's behavior is at times inexplicable, and *good* is not mentioned at all.

Inconsistencies between the two Creations abound.

This doesn't mean the Bible tells about two real Gods. But the Bible does record how different people think about God at different times. The Bible also describes how people understand and follow God in different ways. And most of all, the Bible tracks how God becomes All to human thought and flesh.

Until that day you may find in the story of Eve the message that a woman without her own distinct identity or consciousness is going to be in trouble. Eve's story says if you are asleep to your spiritual identity you will suffer. In fact, if you see her story as a description of consciousness dwelling with a vengeful and inexplicable Deity, it may explain some of the confusion, fear, loneliness and lack of control that you occasionally may feel. It may make you want to find the signposts that point to the all-good, all-powerful *Elohtym* described in the first chapter of Genesis.

What people think about God determines and directs their existence.

The activity of Creator in Genesis 1 reveals itself throughout the Bible and throughout your life. You open to the Bible and to life, take a deep breath, plunge in, dig, get through the rough places, catch a glimpse of the message. You are created in Spirit's image and are made to dwell not in a misty, confusing Eden, but in a distinctly ordered, gender-unbiased universe. No matter how guilty you feel, how far removed from that Creation, God has blessed you and cares for you — which brings us to the message of hope encoded in that first list of "begats" in Genesis 5.

The first two verses of Genesis 5 put together, side by side, words and phrases from the first and second accounts of Creation. We read:

> *This is the book of the generations of Adam. In the day that God created man, in the likeness of God made he him; male and female created he them; and blessed them, and called their name Adam, in the day when they were created.*
>
> (Genesis 5:1–2)

Here is the man, the *male and female* of Genesis 1:27, and Adam, from Genesis 2:7, 22. What follows in Genesis 5:6–32 is the genealogy that is encoded with the message of hope. Man (Adam), Placed (Seth), Incurable Sickness (Enos), Deplorable (Cainan), The Blessed God (Mahaleel), Descends (Jared), Teaching (Enoch), Death Sent Away (Methusaleh), to the Distressed (Lamech), Comfort/Rest (Noah).

This leads us to the Ark and the Flood described in Genesis 6, 7 and 8.

The Flood

Even the most inexperienced Bible reader has heard about Noah, the Ark and the Flood. The Flood (Genesis 7:4, 6) comes as if to wipe away the Adam and Eve story and its repercussions. Humankind can start fresh in consciousness, without the burden of the mistakes of the First Couple. God establishes a covenant — a promise, a contract — with Noah.

Included in the story of Noah, in the midst of the Flood, are more glimpses of the first vision of Creation: God gives Noah *seven days'* warning (Genesis 7:4); the animals are brought into the ark both *male and female* (7:8–9); the ark is lifted above the earth, perhaps into the firmament (Genesis 7:17). The ark represents safety and security, a place evil or danger cannot reach.

> *And God remembered Noah, and every living thing.*
> (Genesis 8:1)

This is the first time the idea of remembering appears in the Bible. This biblical idea of remembering is inextricably linked not only with new beginnings but with pregnancy. If you are interested in conception, with what the Bible says about women having children, this is an appropriate place to curl up again with your Bible and concordance and look up the word *remember.*

This remembering is not nostalgia, not a longing for something that happened in the irretrievable past. Biblical remembering is an active opening-up. You will see, as you look and read the places where *remembered, remembering* and *remembrance* appear, the connection to conception, pregnancy and beginnings. And, along with Noah, you are among *every living thing* that God remembers.

It is Noah who hears the first covenant and sees its evidence, the rainbow (Genesis 9:13). Along with Noah, you are heirs and heiresses of the promise God makes. Every time you see a rainbow you can be reminded of the pact spelled out in Genesis 9. Every time you see a rainbow — whether in a child's drawing or in the sky — you can be assured that there is room for a new beginning. God gives all a second chance.

In a way, it's a promise from God that we can forget about the sorry tale of Adam and Eve. In the story of the Flood, Noah and his wife, and his sons and their wives, are the only people left alive. There may be more reason to consider that we are the descendants, not of Adam and Eve and their unhappy lot, but of the family of Noah and their safe voyage into the elements of the spiritual Creation.

It may not look like it from the story of Adam and Eve or from the sweeping away of all but one family, but the Bible really is a book about infinite, impartial Love. And, yes, there's a happy ending.

But the ending is a long way from Eden and the Flood. And, for women, the passions, adventures, violence, horrors, discoveries and triumphs are just beginning.

Chapter Three

Do As She Tells You

WHAT IF THE BIBLICAL GOD told husbands to obey their wives?

In fact, God does directly tell Abraham — the patriarch of Judaism, Islam and Christianity — to do just what his wife tells him to do.

> *Whatever Sarah says to you, do as she tells you.*
> (Genesis 21:12 *NRSV*)

We will investigate the story of Abraham (Abram) and Sarah (Sarai) and of Hagar who, according to some translations, also marries Abraham. In telling this story the Bible describes women in charge of their own lives. We are exploring the story in depth here to become familiar with how to read a Bible story.

The story, most often read as one of Abraham's faith and God's covenant with men, can be read as a narrative of spiritual power coming to women, working its way through their lives to change the course of history and the people's idea of God. All its progressions and promises are yours as they are Sarah's and Hagar's.

For example:

- God comes to powerless women.
- God controls conception.
- A ticking biological clock is rewound.
- The curse of sorrow in childbirth is reversed.
- Children are a blessing.
- A woman sees God face to face.
- A woman identifies God and gives God a name.
- Laughter is introduced.
- A man weeps for a woman.

More than history

The story begins in Genesis 11, just a chapter and a half after the Flood.

> *Now these are the generations of Terah: Terah begat Abram, Nahor, and Haran; and Haran begat Lot.* (Genesis 11:27)

In one verse it looks as if the story is about some men, the generations of Terah. But the Bible often makes a statement and then leaves out the part that is not relevant for the development of the spiritual idea.

Haran dies, and the text moves right along, focusing ever more sharply on the main point.

> *And Abram and Nahor took them wives: the name of Abram's wife was Sarai.* (Genesis 11:29)

The next verse tells you what the story and its drama will be about.

> *But Sarai was barren; she had no child.* (Genesis 11:30)

But this is also not to be merely a story about a child born to a woman and her husband whose names are to be changed later to Abraham and Sarah. This story speaks to the unfolding of the days of spiritual Creation in human consciousness and to the cost, reward and inevitability of spiritual conception.

Process and cost

The story of Abram and Sarai (whose name means "princess") starts a fascinating progression of biblical women who conceive despite what we think we know of the patterns of biology. In fact, Sarai is an example of a breakthrough in conception. But at this point there is no indication that she wanted children, or whether Abram wanted children.

One of the many ways the Bible is instructive is in the simple telling of the story. We are the ones who fill in the blanks, raising the questions even where there are none. And, as we do, it is our thought that comes to the foreground. We learn what we think, how we feel, what our responses are as we read spare and sometimes fragmentary accounts that seem, on the surface, to be played out against the backdrop of a desert landscape.

Perhaps Sarai liked being a childless princess free to travel with Abram. Perhaps her husband liked it that way too. We may say that the culture of the times demanded children. We may speculate about any number of things. Whatever the case, as their story begins, we know only that she was *married* and *barren.*

> *Now the LORD had said unto Abram, Get thee out of thy country, and from thy kindred, and from thy father's house, unto a land that I will shew thee.* (Genesis 12:1)

The Hebrew in the original text here is *lekh lekha,* meaning "get up and go." The phrase will occur again later in a significant part of Abram's story. It is often important to "get up and go" in order to receive the blessing waiting for you in a rich and full life. For Abram and Sarai, leaving their father's house and starting over is essential. Their move breaks family patterns, and in the process God, rather than any biological mother and father, is revealed as benevolent Parent. Certainly their story will say that God finds you wherever you are on your journey through life.

The Bible: An American Translation continues their story in these easy-to-read words:

> *When he was on the point of entering Egypt, he said to his wife Sarai, "See now, I know that you are such a beautiful woman that when the Egyptians see you, they will say, 'This is his wife,' and then they will kill me in order to keep you. Please say that you are my sister, so that I may be well treated for your sake, and my life spared through you."* (Genesis 12:11–13 AT)

The patriarch asks, he does not tell, his wife to do something. It is her decision to say that she is his sister instead of his wife. She may have said nothing.

How political Sarai's decision was we don't know. And whether or not she found it necessary to remind Abram how much he owed her we also don't know. What we do know at this point is that the patriarch asks her to do this favor for him, thus treating her as an equal and putting him into her debt.

> *The Egyptians saw the woman was very beautiful. Pharaoh's courtiers also saw her, and praised her so highly to Pharaoh that the woman was taken into Pharaoh's household. Abram, too, was well treated for her sake.* (Genesis 12:14–16 AT)

The man is treated well because of the woman.

And Abram owes Sarai his life.

But the Lord strikes Pharaoh and his household with disease. The Pharaoh is angry:

> *"What a way for you to treat me! Why did you not tell me that she was your wife? Why did you say, 'She is my sister,' and let me marry her? Well, there is your wife; take her and begone!"*
>
> (Genesis 12:19 *AT*)

Abram, who receives much wealth from Pharaoh for leaving, is certainly the richer for this encounter, and we hear nothing from Sarai. It may mean that it goes without saying that at this point she is the pivotal factor in the couple's mutual journey. And there is no mention that either Abram or Sarai suffers for or from this episode. It's as if they can't do anything wrong. In fact, they have so much in terms of flocks, herds and tents that the land can't bear them all. Eventually, Abram offers his nephew Lot first choice of all the lands, and they divide the wealth amicably. Lot chooses all the plain of Jordan (Genesis 13:1–12).

Passing Sarai off as Abram's sister happens again later, but for now, the Lord makes a startling announcement to a childless couple. He tells Abram that he and his descendants will possess all the lands of earth:

> *And I will make thy seed as the dust of the earth: so that if a man can number the dust of the earth, then shall thy seed also be numbered.* (Genesis 13:16)

Seeds and stars

The reader will surely note that in this promise there are words from both the first story of Creation and the second — *seed* and *dust: the seed within itself* from the third day of Creation in the first chapter of Genesis and *dust*, the stuff of which Adam was made as recounted in the second chapter of Genesis.

Here is a glimmer of reforming the Adam story. This beginning glimpse in consciousness is a promise that is going to evolve. There are stages of consciousness involved in the fulfillment of this promise.

One of those stages is communion. As you read the evolving story in your Bible, you see that Abram encounters the king of Salem (peace), Melchizedek, who brings him *bread* and *wine* and who blesses him and his God (Genesis 14:18–20).

One way to read your Bible is to stop at this point and use your concordance to look up *bread* and *wine*. You see the richness involved even in what seems to be the simplest progression of events. *Bread* and *wine* are a timeless part of human life. Their spiritual signification leads to glimpses of the profound provision available at each stage and state of consciousness. A study of *bread* and *wine* may drive you to the kitchen; it may also lead you to the abundance implicit in this encounter, this meal.

Rejoining Abram, one sees that after the communion and blessing he has a vision. In this vision, after this communion, Abram hears a new definition of God and a new description of the promise to him.

I am thy shield, and thy exceeding great reward. (Genesis 15:1)

And the promise now has evolved.

And he brought him forth abroad, and said, Look now toward heaven, and tell the stars, if thou be able to number them: and he said unto him, So shall thy seed be. (Genesis 15:5)

Now Abram's seed will not be made from *dust* as Adam was. It's as if we are to see that thought starts with one idea and moves beyond that idea into a broader one. There is still the *third-day* reference to the *seed,* but the relationship is now not to dust but to the *fourth-day* creation of stars.

There is a hint, a mingling here of the *third* and *fourth days,* figuratively of seeds attaching themselves to stars. We see echoes of this later in Matthew 2:1–2, when the star appears to the wise men and leads them to the manger and the baby Jesus.

No longer children of dust as in the second creation, Abram's heirs will now be numberless children of *light.* Things are looking up.

God's spiritual Creation is revealing itself to human thought. Abram's consciousness has moved from one phase, one day, of spiritual Creation to the next.

You can apply that progressive revelation of spiritual Creation to your life. It's an adventure to discover that each step of your experience has more spiritual enlightenment than the last. There is an authentic and timeless order of meaning and substance to be found in recognizing stages of thought as falling into or bordering on the *days* of spiritual Creation.

A hint that will help you see your experience and thought as progressive and unfolding is to be grateful for how far you have come. Don't worry about how far you have to go.

If we are meant to learn from biblical experience, then we may learn from Abram's experience that Spirit's promises come true, but that fulfillment does not always come with the first dawning of an idea. Often it does come with the first acceptance of an idea but sometimes — in the Bible and in your life — it takes months and years for promises to come to fruition.

The reader will remember as she reads on in Genesis that *fourth* is a feminine word in Hebrew, and thus it may be significant that after the promise of Genesis 15:5 we hear from Sarai that she does want a child.

And to that end Sarai makes a decision.

Consequences

Sarai says to Abram, *the LORD has kept me from having children.* Her solution is not to go to God but rather she suggests that Abram, her husband, marry her maid, Hagar, so that *perhaps I can build a family through her* (Genesis 16:1, 2 *NIV*).

What must she have been thinking? you ask yourself. Or you may think that was then and this is now. But what about surrogate motherhood today? While Sarai's offer to marry Hagar off to Abram may seem selfless or even stupid to modern readers, while it may seem to the reader that trouble is bound to ensue, the Bible (contrary to present human notions that throughout its pages women are judged) passes no judgment on her actions. It simply tells the story.

He slept with Hagar, and she conceived. When she knew she was pregnant, she began to despise her mistress.
(Genesis 16:4 *NIV*)

As quickly as the Bible has told us what happens, Sarai tells Abram that she recognizes she has made a big mistake. She feels an injustice has been done, that Abram is to blame. Sarai asks the Lord to judge the matter directly (Genesis 16:5).

Even if one reads the accounts of Eve and Sarai to say that women act importunately, unwisely, one can also read their accounts to say that women are first to see and admit mistakes. Sarai now recognizes that it is God, not her husband, who can correct the mistake. She is in a long line of women who to this day ask the Lord, not their husbands, to take care of a tricky situation and help deal with the consequences.

Abram, too, recognizes that it is not up to him to resolve this situation. He tells Sarai that it is up to her to figure it out. She has been and is in charge. She is responsible for her own conscious understanding of God. One way to miss this profound biblical point is to read into the Bible our limited knowledge of the history of the times.

For example, there is a widely held belief that women of Sarai's time had no legal rights or status. But the story of Sarai and Abram is not the story of a woman with no legal rights or status. As for polygamy, Sarai was wife to Pharaoh at Abram's suggestion that she declare herself his sister. Abram's taking a second wife is the result of Sarai's prompting. Here polygamy is a two-way street and not just the right of a man.

As one reads the Bible stories as they are written one sees that the patriarch was not the absolute ruler of his household — father, provider, king, judge and husband responsible for everything and everybody.

In the story of Sarai's giving Hagar to Abram some readers have surmised that Hagar was a princess herself and came with Sarai as part of the deal from Pharaoh when he sent the couple away. But we don't know that from the Bible. We don't know how friendly the women were before Sarai's decision to send Hagar to Abram's bed. What the Bible does make clear, though, is that after conceiving, Hagar despised Sarai (Genesis 16:4).

What do you think about this story? Do you think this reflects badly on women? It's possible to look at this story as a warning. Giving your husband to another woman so that you can have what you think you want is not a bed of roses. How can we not expect Hagar to despise Sarai? Hagar may not want to be pregnant. She may not want to have been used. She may feel now that she, not Sarai, has the power. She is, after all to be mother of Abram's child. The Bible may be instructing us not to be naive. Or to wait on God.

We simply do not know the cause of Hagar's hatred toward Sarai. The Bible feels no need to analyze Hagar's emotions. Human reaction is often inexplicable, and that may well be enough for us to know. In fact, that may well be the point.

But not surprisingly, in a home where one woman despises another, there is trouble. Sarai, on the defensive, is hard on Hagar, and so Hagar, not a long-suffering martyr but an independent woman, runs away from the abuse.

Angels and powerless women

For the first time in the Bible an angel appears — not to a man, but to a woman. To a suffering woman. To a woman alone (Genesis 16:7). Whether she is a runaway, a victim or a co-conspirator is of no importance to this telling. What is important is that the first (and certainly not the last) biblical appearance of an angel is to a woman alone.

The angel of the Lord comes to Hagar beside a spring of *waters*. You already know, as you read Hagar's story, that *water* illustrates Spirit's presence.

"*Where have you come from and where are you going?*" (Genesis 16:8 *NIV*) the angel asks her. Here are questions for the ages. Ask yourself, "Where have I come from? Where am I going?"

Thinking we come from Eve is not much help. Reminding ourselves that the answer may be found in the Spirit and spiritual Creation, we see that the answer is: coming from *ruach Elohiym* and going only in that goodness and blessedness.

No point here in long-winded self-justification, and so Hagar, like Eve, like Sarai, simply tells what happened: "*I'm running away from my mistress Sarai*" (Genesis 16:8 *NIV*).

The angel tells her to return to Sarai and gives Hagar the same quantitative promise that has been unfolding to Abram (Genesis 13:16; 15:5) — the promise that her descendants will be too numerous to count (Genesis 16:10).

In addition, Hagar hears, *Behold, thou art with child, and shalt bear a son, and shalt call his name Ishmael; because the LORD hath heard thy affliction* (Genesis 16:11).

Hagar is only the first in a long line of biblical women whose children are announced or named by angelic representatives. As you look in your concordance for *angel,* you will follow the line from Hagar through to the other women in the Bible whose children are announced by angels.

A woman names God

Hagar names *the LORD who spoke to her El-roi (a God who can be seen)*. She says, *I have actually seen God, and am still alive after seeing him* (Genesis 16:13 *AT*).

The narrative says that Hagar sees an angel, but then quotes her as saying that she sees *the LORD*. In many places throughout the Bible this happens to both women and men. First it looks as if (or sounds as if) an angel is standing there speaking. Then the angel becomes the Lord. Angels lead to God.

Hagar has Abram's son, and she does call him Ishmael (Genesis 16:15 *AT*).

New names

And Abram is ninety-nine years old. The Lord appears to him yet again and announces for the seventh time that his descendants will be a great nation and that a covenant is about to be made between them. And God re-names him Abraham (Genesis 17:1–8).

And God tells Abraham that he and every male in his house — including servants — must be circumcised. Male children are to be circumcised on the eighth day (Genesis 17:10–14).

> *As for Sarai thy wife, thou shalt not call her name Sarai, but Sarah shall her name be. And I will bless her, and give thee a son also of her: yea, I will bless her, and she shall be a mother of nations; kings of people shall be of her.* (Genesis 17:15–16)

And then Abraham falls on his face laughing (Genesis 17:17). Sarah is now ninety.

But Abraham's God knows nothing of biological clocks.

The name *Sarah* means "abundance" as in Genesis 1:21 where the *waters* bring forth life *abundantly*.

But Abraham wishes rather, *O that Ishmael might live before thee!* (Genesis 17:18).

God doesn't answer that right away but instead repeats that Sarah will have a son and *thou shalt call his name Isaac* (Genesis 17:19). *Isaac* means "laughter." The joke is on Abraham. Naming the child "laughter" may indicate that, among other things, Abraham's God has a sense of humor and that there is a correlation between human response, human emotion and one's perception of God.

And as for Ishmael, I have heard thee (Genesis 17:20). What greater words of comfort can a parent hear than that God has heard? *I have blessed him,* God says.

> *And will make him fruitful, and will multiply him exceedingly; twelve princes shall he beget, and I will make him a great nation. But my covenant will I establish with Isaac.*
>
> (Genesis 17:20–21)

These pronouncements from God can't get much more specific. It's hard to think of anything more specific than circumcision. That same day Abraham and Ishmael and all the males of Abraham's house are circumcised. The Bible tells us twice of that event and later commands, *Circumcise therefore the foreskins of your heart, and be no more stiffnecked* (Deuteronomy 10:16).

Now, in more than physicality Abraham is a changed man and Sarah, as well, is a changed woman. The altered dimension is indicated by the next biblical story, which begins: *The LORD appeared to him in the oak grove of Mamre as he sat in his tent door in the heat of the day* (Genesis 18:1 *Tyn*). The eighteenth chapter of Genesis is rich with the essence of the biblical approach to life and God. Let's consider some of the story's spiritual implications as it is laid out in the first eight verses.

The Lord appears (Genesis 18:1). All that happens is in the presence of the Lord. This tent has more than one meaning. Not just cloth and poles, not just the home of an ancient wandering nomad, this tent where Abraham sits — half in and half out — symbolizes a larger context. The word *tent* also means "house," as in the Twenty-third Psalm, verse 6, where *I shall dwell in the house of the LORD,* means "understanding" or "consciousness."

Abraham is neither in nor out of the tent but in the door — the place of coming in and going out. There is the added suggestion here that he was half in his body, his *house,* and half in the *house* of the Lord. It's not an uncommon experience to be so caught up in meditation, prayer or activity that one forgets one's body for a time.

In this state Abraham lifts up his eyes (a biblical signal the story is going to move into another dimension) and sees three men come unexpectedly and uninvited to visit (Genesis 18:2). What do we do when strangers come to the door unexpectedly and uninvited?

Abraham leaps up and bows himself to the ground. Abraham does what we generally believe only women do. He serves. He extends hospitality. He begs the men to stay, gets them water to wash their feet, bids them rest under a tree, fetches them bread to comfort their hearts (Genesis 18:3–5). The importance of hospitality is illustrated.

Abraham's relationship with Sarah has taken a turn. He doesn't consult with her or ask her permission to entertain strangers. In fact, he runs to her saying that she should get three measures of meal and bake cakes for the guests, then runs to the herd to get a calf for meat, takes butter, milk and the calf that has been cooked and sets it all before the men while he stands beside them as they eat under the tree (Genesis 18:7–8). One can only think Sarah must have loved the eager and humble boy in Abraham at this moment.

The first thing they say is, *Where is Sarah, thy wife?* (Genesis 18:9).

No thank yous. No discussion of the weather or of politics or economy. Biblical people don't engage in meandering conversations. They get right to the point.

Abraham says that Sarah is *in the tent*. It's a thought-provoking contrast to his own sitting *in the door* of his *tent*. And the men then repeat what we know Abraham has already heard God say — there will be a child. Next year. There is more laughter. Abraham laughs, and so does Sarah, who overhears the news while *in the tent*.

After I am waxed old shall I have pleasure, my lord being old also? she says (Genesis 18:12).

Any notions one might have that the Bible is against sex ought to be dispelled by Sarah's description of the act as pleasure, which, in a Hebrew translation, is "lust." The Lord continues the dialogue with Abraham asking him, *did Sarah laugh, saying, Shall I of a surety bear a child, which am old? Is any thing too hard for the LORD?* (Genesis 18:13–14).

And for the first time Sarah doesn't answer directly. She denies that she laughed.

For she was afraid, the Bible explains (Genesis 18:15).

If you think you can hide anything at all from Spirit, look at the next lines, where the Lord says, in response, *Oh yes; but you did laugh* (Genesis 18:15).

This Lord, with whom women converse easily and who converses easily with them, knows everything. And the Lord does not punish or chide Sarah for her denial. Instead, the men then stood up and looked toward Sodom.

Abraham goes with them *on the way* (Genesis 18:16). We will see so much more of *the way* that it is worth noting here. (There are 664 biblical references to *the way* and all merit exploring.)

Just as nothing about Sarah can be withheld from the Lord, the Lord has a discussion with himself about whether anything — such as the future of Sodom and Gomorrah — can be withheld from Abraham.

For some time Abraham questions and negotiates with the Lord about saving the territory. If there are fifty righteous, will you save it, Abraham wants to know? Yes, the Lord agrees. How about forty-five? Forty? And on down to ten. Many powerful concepts are involved in this dialogue and one we will pick up later is Abraham's negotiating with the Lord (Genesis 18:17–32).

Another school of thought

The Bible is interested in simultaneous time and not merely chronological time, so the narrative often interrupts one story to tell another, the threads of which have already been laid or will be picked up later. This story of God's intervention in the fleshly affairs of women and their wombs is interrupted by the intervention of the story of Sodom and Gomorrah, with the story of the wife and daughters of Lot (Genesis 19).

A brief sketch of the widely known tale includes the destruction of Sodom and Gomorrah, as well as Lot's wife looking back and turning into a pillar of salt. There are many levels to this story. On one level the story is about the destruction of iniquity. On another level the message to women can be read: forget what is behind, don't look back. Move on. Keep going. Looking back can paralyze you.

Lot's daughters, who don't look back, survive and live in a cave with their father. Thinking they are the only people left on earth and feeling responsible for re-populating the planet, they decide to get their father drunk. They have sex with him, in turn, on two successive evenings. They both become pregnant. The elder daughter delivers a son, Moab, and the younger, a son named Benammi.

We will see later that Ruth, a female descendant of Moab, is an absolutely essential part of the prophetic line of Israel. A circle of women is being drawn and a message sent that not only do women take things into their own hands, but it is important to look forward rather than back.

There is no punishment for Lot's daughters' doing what they thought was the only thing to do under the circumstances. Limited as their concept was, as full of self-justification as it might possibly be, as pointed as the reference to incest is, there is still no judgment and, in fact, their progeny are essential to biblical history. Finger-pointing is out as far as the Spirit is concerned.

Back to the future

As you read your Bible, you will see that the story then cuts back to Abraham and Sarah (Genesis 20).

Sarah, still beautiful at ninety (have women today limited them-selves to beauty only of the early decades?), is again passed off by Abraham as his sister, this time to Abimelech, whose name means, "My Father is King." Again we don't know what, if anything, Sarah says. But in a dream God explains to Abimelech that Abraham is a prophet and is married to Sarah.

Confronted by Abimelech, Abraham explains his misrepresenta-tion by saying that first of all he didn't think the fear of God was in this place, and so out of fear himself, he hid his marital relationship with Sarah. In fact, the biblical God is in all the action and speaks to men and women without regard to clan or tribe.

Second, Abraham explains to the king, Sarah is not only his wife but his half-sister — daughter of his father but not his mother. As in the earlier story of Abraham's passing Sarai (Sarah) off to Pharaoh as his sister and not his wife, Abraham, though he misrepresented (or lied), comes out of the episode again unpunished and again wealth-ier. Why he juggles the complete and literal fact of his relationship to Sarai is explained by the Bible only in Abraham's words. In the first incident he asks Sarai to say she is his sister so he will be well treated for her sake. In the second he says that he thought the fear of God wasn't *in this place,* and *they will kill me because of my wife* (Genesis 20:11 *TNK*).

Abimelech says to Sarah, *I have given thy brother a thousand pieces of silver,* and he adds, *you are completely vindicated* (Genesis 20:16 *NIV*). No guilt, shame or blame for Sarah.

God and wombs

At this point there is no question that conception is unmistakably the province of God. Genesis 20:17–18 tells us of God's *closing* and then, through Abraham's prayer, reopening the wombs of the women of the house of Abimelech. And then, further, *the LORD visited Sarah as he had said, and the LORD did unto Sarah as he had spoken* (Genesis 21:1).

The Creator keeps promises.

And where Eve's experience carries a curse, Sarah's is blessed.

And where she once worried about what others thought, once believed she would be a laughingstock if she bore a child in her nineties, Sarah now rejoices as she plays with the word *laugh*.

> *Sarah said, God hath made me to laugh, so that all that hear will laugh with me. And she said, Who would have said unto Abraham, that Sarah should have given children suck? for I have borne him a son in his old age.* (Genesis 21:6–7)

After Isaac is weaned Sarah sees *the son of Hagar the Egyptian, which she had borne unto Abraham, mocking* (Genesis 21:9).

She asks Abraham to get rid of both Hagar and Ishmael.

It nearly breaks Abraham's heart.

He is grieved.

In fact, Sarah is the first to figure out what is to be done in a very, very rocky situation.

It is at this emotional low point for a conflicted Abraham that God tells him to obey his wife: *in all that Sarah hath said unto thee, hearken unto her voice* (Genesis 21:12).

God assures Abraham that Hagar's son will be a *great nation* even though Hagar faces what appears to be an uncertain future (Genesis 21:13). Where before Hagar ran away from Sarah, now she is sent off, with Abraham taking *bread* and a bottle of *water* and putting it on Hagar's shoulder (Genesis 21:14).

What Abraham gives Hagar is that which is essential to life — *bread* and *water*. Read literally *bread* and *water* seem to be basic prisoner's rations. But read with an eye to the spiritual symbolism we recognize the importance of *bread* and *water*. We have already seen *bread* play an important part in Abraham's communion meeting with Melchizedek, and we will see further into the Bible that *bread* continues to play a role in communion (Matthew 26:26).

Then Abraham takes Ishmael and gives the child to her. Abraham is there for Hagar, caring, touching, holding, even as he is torn, even as he feels he must do this harsh-seeming thing that Sarah and God have told him to do. He cares deeply and tenderly despite the fact that it was never his idea in the first place to make Hagar his wife or have a child by her.

When we see the Bible says that *bread* and *water* in their spiritual signification are supplied to Ishmael, when we see how grieved Abraham is at having to send Hagar and Ishmael off, we have much to weigh. This story, which began with Sarah's decision to marry her husband to Hagar *so that she might have children by her,* deserves all the deepest prayer and humility we can find within ourselves.

No observation, no sophisticated political knowledge here can touch the weight or contemporary echoes of this biblical account. Your gut instinct has to tell you that God is providing for everyone, that there is provision for both of Abraham's sons, *water* and *bread* for all.

What to do?

At this point in the story things look a mess. Sarah, the mother of Judaism and Christianity, and Abraham, the father of Judaism, Christianity and Islam, are in a muddle, and Hagar, the mother of Islam, is wandering in the wilderness of Beer-sheba ("the well of the oath").

But we've read ahead to Revelation and know that the woman and her child who are being pursued are lifted up on eagle's wings into the *wilderness* for protection and not for punishment. Think of eagle's wings as a metaphor for Spirit lifting women up; such a vision elucidates what is happening to Hagar and what can happen to any woman, any time, anywhere.

For those who enjoy significant detail as well as metaphor, Abraham later will make a pact with Abimelech at this same well and dwell there still later. His son will have an important encounter there, and his grandson too. But Hagar is there first. Now her *water* is gone and she casts her son under one of the shrubs. She goes *a good way off* because she doesn't want to see the death of her child.

She *lifted up her voice, and wept* (Genesis 21:16).

Who wouldn't? To all appearances she and her child are serious victims. Marrying Abram was done in obedience to Sarai. Bearing a child was done in obedience to an angel of the Lord. Now she is sitting weeping in the *wilderness* with her child who, she fears, is near death. It's a stark moment.

The link between all mothers and their children is illustrated here. She cries. *And God heard the voice of the lad. . . .*

Nothing has been said about the child's crying or speaking. The mother's tears get God's attention: *. . . and the angel of God called to Hagar out of heaven, and said unto her, What aileth thee Hagar?*

She doesn't have to answer: *. . . fear not; for God hath heard the voice of the lad where he is* (Genesis 21:17).

The angel tells her what she was told earlier in the story, *fear not*. Has she forgotten that the first step in seeing your way out of a nightmare situation is to *fear not?*

If Hagar, in her extreme circumstances, couldn't remember that she had earlier seen an angel who told her not to fear, and if she couldn't remember that she saw God, who told her that her son would be the father of nations, then perhaps we shouldn't be too hard on ourselves when we fall apart. Perhaps we should write *fear not* on our doorposts and key chains, in ink on our palms, in our Bibles and journals and in our hearts.

> *Fear not; for God hath heard the voice of the lad where he is. Arise, lift up the lad, and hold him in thine hand; for I will make him a great nation. And God opened her eyes, and she saw a well of water; and she went, and filled the bottle with water, and gave the lad to drink.* (Genesis 21:17–19).

Seeking and finding

God opened Hagar's eyes, and she saw the well of *water* that was already there. *And God was with the lad; and he grew, and dwelt in the wilderness, and became an archer . . . and his mother took him a wife out of the land of Egypt* (Genesis 21:20–21).

As you read for yourself, you may ponder the question posed: Is losing something actually finding it? Look at the story of Sarah, Hagar and Abraham and see how often loss precedes gain. Losing her immediate position in the household looked to be a great loss to Hagar. But despite the short-term fear and loss, Spirit provides abundantly for everyone involved. Later, one of Hagar's granddaughters marries one of Sarah's grandsons.

The story of Sarah and Hagar and Abraham illustrates a rich complexity of behavior. We have been told repeatedly to *fear not*. We have been shown again and again that God's spiritual Creation is unveiled to human thought in specific form. That Spirit is Creator and Parent in Sarah and Abraham and Hagar's story. We have been shown that God takes care of women and their children. And we know for a fact that the Bible says God comes to where you are — no matter where that may be.

The sacrifice

What kind of a father would even dream of sacrificing his child? What kind of a God is it, some have said, that would even ask you to sacrifice your child? A surface reading of Genesis 22:1–19 can cause a shudder.

The story of the almost-sacrifice is fraught with symbols and prefigurations. And it must be read through those symbols to see what the story — other than the traditional and textually oversimplistic "Abraham had faith in God" — is saying.

Read in the light of what you already know about Abraham's life and relationship to his God, read in the light of the first chapter of Creation, the story of Abraham's taking Isaac to the mountain is not a story about a temperamental male God testing His favorite person on earth. Instead, the idea that God demands human sacrifice dies in this story. This story is about timeless reality, about Spirit's care for each child, about the trust of a parent in that Spirit.

By the time this familiar tale unfolds, Abraham and Sarah have had a lot of practice in trusting God. They left their ancestral home and found a fuller, richer life. God has already taken care of Ishmael. Abraham has by now a certain confidence in his relationship to God. Everything God has told him to do has worked out for Abraham's benefit.

Once again Abraham is told *lekh lekha*, "get up and go."

This is the second time Abraham hears these words, which should suggest to the reader that familiar territory is ahead — God has a terrific and improbable plan.

On the *third day* of his journey, Abraham raises his eyes and sees a sanctuary. The *third day* again. The spiritual Creation clue. *Moriah*, the land to which Abraham travels, means "seen of God." Translate it for yourself and see that although there is a literal, geographical journey going on here, there is also a shift into another dimension.

If you take chronological time out of the picture and replace it with simultaneous time, you see that there is a sanctuary in the third day and that the entire process is "seen of God."

Compare this story to others that talk about the *third day*. Take chronological time out of the picture and you can see — in simultaneous time — Abraham putting the wood for the burnt offering on the back of Isaac. When Isaac questions the endeavor, Abraham says God will *provide* a lamb for the burnt offering. One of the biblical names for Jesus is Lamb of God. And the key word here is *provide*. Sarah and Abraham's God provides, giving forth life *abundantly*.

A careful reading of this story reveals that the supposed sacrifice of a child is not, nor was ever going to be, about the sacrifice of Isaac. What is sacrificed?

Be sure that you look, as you read this story, at Genesis 22, verse 14: *And Abraham called the name of that place Jehovah-jireh: as it is said to this day, In the mount of the LORD it shall be seen.*

Go up to the mountain (the high place), and *it shall be seen.* Not, "go up to the mountain for a useless trip." Not, "go up to the mountain and have your heart broken," or "kill your child." Look at verse 19 in Genesis 22. See there that Abraham went and dwelt at Beer-sheba ("the well of the oath") — where Hagar and Ishmael were nurtured and saved. The story of saving — not sacrifice — has come full circle.

There are many opinions and reactions to this story. What Abraham and Isaac saw on the mountain is only sketched. Read against a background of Abraham's life as told in the Bible, read as prefiguration, there is much there to ponder. Some women may wonder what Sarah was doing while her husband and son went to the mountain. If one thinks she was a powerless piece of property, then she must have been anguished, distraught and furious. But if one assumes that she knew from experience that God takes care of children and powerless women, then she wasn't worried.

Years later, when Sarah dies, Abraham weeps and wails for her. Though her body is buried near Mamre at Machpelah (Genesis 23:19), her name lives on in the Bible:

That is, They which are the children of the flesh, these are not the children of God: but the children of the promise are counted for the seed. For this is the word of promise, At this time will I come, and Sarah shall have a son. (Romans 9:8–9)

Fulfilled promise. The consciousness that knows God does fulfill promises to women. New birth. The consciousness that nothing is impossible to God. Creation revealed to complex consciousness regardless of gender. That's what the story of Sarah, Hagar and Abraham is about as much as it is about anything.

And there are more words of promise, more sons and daughters, more development of the idea of God's nature to come in the lives of women and their children. Their lives and experiences will spare you some harsh times and give you some hints beyond *fear not* about Bible facts you can apply to your life today.

Chapter Four

A Gathering of Women

W<small>HAT IF BIBLICAL WOMEN</small> are not isolated, solitary figures on a desert landscape but vitally linked to us today in the struggle for the vindication of the rights of women?

Demythologizing Eve is seldom done in a single stroke. Part of the process of demythologizing Eve — and the role and nature of women in the Bible — is to search out connections, histories, women's experiences.

Certainly reading the Bible in the light of the lives of the women restores to us the depth of experience, joy and sorrow, the sacrifice made by those who have been on the path before us. Biblical women are not veiled non-entities trailing behind husbands and camels. They certainly have their own relationships to God, and they have rights.

Rebekah, for example, has the right to decide whom and when she marries.

Abraham has sent his emissary on a mission to find and bring back a wife for Isaac. The emissary is concerned that the woman might not consent or agree to be Isaac's wife and to leave her own land. If the woman does not consent or agree to return, Abraham says, then his emissary is released from any obligation for the mission (Genesis 24:1–8). There would have been no reason for wondering whether the woman would return with the emissary if women had no rights to determine their own marital status.

We find Rebekah in the land of Sarah's sister-in-law, Milcah. Coming out to the well in Genesis 24:15, Rebekah is seen by the emissary, who had asked the Lord to make clear which woman is the right woman.

"May it be that when I say to a girl, 'Please let down your jar that I may have a drink,' and she says, 'Drink, and I'll water

your camels too'— let her be the one you have chosen for your servant Isaac." (Genesis 24:14 *NIV*)

Immediately, Rebekah appears and offers the servant exactly the kindnesses he seeks in exactly the words he has requested. Only one of the conclusions that may be drawn from this encounter is that Rebekah, a woman, knew where to be and what to say. The Bible repeats this placing of woman at the right place at the right time through the Resurrection and beyond.

There is plenty of straw and feed at home, and also room to spend the night, Rebekah says (Genesis 24:25 *TNK*).

At first blush this may not seem like much more than traditional hospitality, but in biblical terms this line prefigures the manger — straw, room to lodge. The story of Rebekah has word-based connections to Mary's time in the manger as she delivered her son, Jesus. In other ways, Rebekah's story has connections to the stories of Eve, Sarah, Rachel, Tamar, Miriam, Hannah, Ruth and Naomi. As you read further into these women's stories, you will see the connections. The lives of biblical women are woven together not only by family relations but by clearly marked symbols and similarities impossible to overlook.

Rebekah's family pleads with her to stay with them a little longer and asks, *Will you go with this man? I will go,* she says (Genesis 24:58 *TNK*), an indication of her own freedom to choose and a precursor to what Ruth says to Naomi: *Whither thou goest, I will go* (Ruth 1:16).

Rebekah goes. Her family's blessing is on her: *Thou art our sister, be thou the mother of thousands of millions, and let thy seed possess the gate of those which hate them* (Genesis 24:60).

This is another reference to the triumph of woman's *seed* over hatred first described in the story of Eve. Without reading past the first half of the first book of the Bible, we find references to the ultimate triumph of woman over hatred.

What is seen

Isaac is taking a walk in the field in the evening and lifts up his eyes. He sees camels coming. Rebekah, riding one of those camels, lifts up her eyes and sees Isaac (Genesis 24:63–64)

He sees camels.

She sees him.

She sees one thing, and he sees another. This is not to weep or foam over. It may well be profitable instruction. Men and women may perceive the same situation differently and do not have to see the same thing at the same time.

Rebekah, the story says, goes with Isaac into Sarah's tent, and *he loved her; and Isaac was comforted after his mother's death* (Genesis 24:67).

Rebekah has a husband who loves her. As you read her story in your Bible you will note, however, that there is no mention of whether or not she, in return, loves him. You will note also the mention of his being comforted after the death of his mother. A single biblical sentence speaks volumes about their relationship.

Biology

The narration says that Rebekah is *barren,* as Sarah was *barren. Because Rebecca had no children, Isaac prayed to the LORD for her* (Genesis 25:21 *GNB*).

Getting what you ask for is not a new concept. Biblical men and women get what they ask for. God reflects back to Isaac his own request — *the LORD answered his prayer* — and their monogamous marriage produces twin sons. And *Isaac preferred Esau and Rebecca preferred Jacob* (Genesis 25:28 *GNB*). Another bittersweet, poignant description of human nature in a few words.

Esau sells Jacob his birthright for a little bit of food (Genesis 25:29–34). Then comes a famine, and then comes another of those biblical reprises (Genesis 26:1–10).

God tells Isaac to go to Egypt and dwell there and receive the promise of his father Abraham. Abimelech is still the king, and Isaac tells Abimelech that Rebekah is his sister in just the same way that his father did about his mother. And Abimelech rewards him the same way that Abraham was rewarded. Not only do we know Rebekah is not even Isaac's half-sister, but Abimelech is not as easily fooled this time; and when he sees Rebekah and Isaac *making love,* he deduces that Rebekah is Isaac's wife. Abimelech rebukes Isaac for this deception saying, *"One of my men might easily have slept with your wife, and you would have been responsible for our guilt"* (Genesis 26:10 *GNB*).

Even if we have a helpful history of parental relations to God, it seems from this account that each generation learns and receives

God's promises directly. That may mean improving on our parents' past experience; it may mean leaving that experience altogether; it may mean cashing in on the blessings. We live it all for ourselves — whoever or whatever our parents are or have been.

Esau marries Judith and Basemath, women from another country with another manner of worship. *They made life miserable for Isaac and Rebecca* (Genesis 26:35 *GNB*). Parental anguish over a child's spouse is not ancient history but as contemporary a dilemma as one can find.

So too is Rebekah's involvement with the son she loves most. The story of her favorite, Jacob, pretending to be Esau in order to obtain the blessing of primogeniture is well known. At Rebekah's urging (*do what I say,* she says [Genesis 27:8 *GNB*]) and with her full support, Jacob puts a hairy skin over his body, and Isaac, in failing eyesight, thinks it is his hairy son Esau and so gives to Jacob the patriarchal blessing that was the right of the firstborn (Genesis 27:1–29).

We will see unequivocally the laws of biological primogeniture are not the laws of the Lord of the Bible. *Firstborn* applies not to the first biological child, as far as God is concerned. It applies to whom the Lord chooses. And the Lord often chooses not the "good" child, but the one with dubious behavior. Story after story in the Bible repeats this message.

We see as we read further that, although Rebekah's instincts are in line with God, Jacob has denied his own identity to get this traditional blessing. As a consequence of his own actions he will spend years being deceived and years working his way out of deception.

When Esau — like Adam and Eve's first son, Cain — decides to kill his brother, Rebekah hears of it before it can happen.

Strategies for survival

We know Esau's plan will fail because neither Adam and Eve nor their children are the paradigm for God's men and women. The *seed* of Adam and Eve has been replaced by the seed of Sarah and Abraham and of Rebekah and Isaac.

Rebekah, who knows this at some level, has been, like Sarah, involving herself with God's plan. As a protection to her sons, she thinks to send Jacob to her brother Laban's. Later Moses' mother will place him in the river in an ark for safety (Exodus 2:3). Mary will take her child to Egypt for protection (Matthew 2:13–15). Sending or taking one's child away from danger is biblical wisdom and often contemporary good judgment.

Rebekah gets her one son away from the other by telling her husband that she is tired of her daughters-in-law and that she'd rather be dead than to see Jacob have a wife like Esau's. Any woman who has ever said, "I'd rather be dead than . . . " can relate to Rebekah. Isaac — thinking it's his own idea — sends Jacob to Rebekah's brother, Laban, where we meet Rachel (Genesis 28:1–5).

Marriage and crucifixion

The story of Rachel, Rebekah's niece and daughter-in-law, is not just a story of love at first sight. It is that and more — duplicity, money, mandrakes, maids, childbearing and death. Moreover, Rachel's story prefigures the crucifixion of Jesus of Nazareth (Matthew 26–28, Mark 14–16, Luke 22–24, John 18–21). It is not a story about a docile young piece of property who becomes the mother of some of the sons of Jacob. As in the crucifixion, the story of Rachel is a story of timeless elements: love, sacrifice, rebirth and more love.

To read Rachel's story as a prefiguration of crucifixion is one of the demanding ways a text can be read and a reminder that the Bible is self-referential. Seeing this relationship deepens our conception of women's significance in the Bible and lets us know how much it sometimes costs to love.

The story begins:

Then Jacob went on his journey, and came to the land of the people of the east. As he looked, he saw a well in the field and three flocks of sheep lying there beside it; for out of that well the flocks were watered. The stone on the well's mouth was large, and when all the flocks were gathered there, the shepherds would roll the stone from the mouth of the well, and water the sheep, and put the stone back in its place on the mouth of the well. (Genesis 29:1–3 NRSV)

As you look through the first twelve verses of this chapter, translate the text into a deeper and broader landscape.

You are at the *waters*. You see that Rachel is a shepherd (Genesis 29:9), as is David later (1 Samuel 16:19), and as Jesus is the *good shepherd* (John 10:11).

Flock is used often to refer to people. After Jacob sees Rachel, he rolls the stone away from the mouth of the well and *waters the flock* (Genesis 29:10). Jacob rolls the stone from the well's mouth as the stone will be rolled from the tomb of Lazarus (John 11:38–41) and the tomb of Jesus (Luke 24:2).

Then Jacob kissed Rachel, and broke into tears (Genesis 29:11). Jesus, too, will weep (John 11:35).

Jacob reveals to Rachel his identity. He tells her he is Rebekah's son.

The price of deception

So Jacob served seven years for Rachel, and they seemed to him but a few days because of the love he had for her.

(Genesis 29:20 *NRSV*)

Some might complain about a seven-year wait; others would only wish for that kind of devotion from a suitor.

Jacob, who used duplicity to secure the blessing of the firstborn, suffers poetic justice when, after seven years of working for Rachel, he is given Rachel's sister, Leah, on his wedding night (Genesis 29:16–26).

He works *seven years* more for Rachel (Genesis 29:27–28). The reader can't help but see the sisters' situation as reflective of the struggle between Jacob and Esau. But after seven days Jacob and Rachel consummate their marriage.

The story tells of much maneuvering between the sisters and their handmaids, Zilpah and Bilhah, all four of whom have children by Jacob (Genesis 29:29–35:23).

The story of Leah, Rachel, Zilpah and Bilhah can only be imagined. Four women, one husband, assorted children, a scheming father, mandrakes in exchange for a night with Jacob, a clash of cultures — it's a struggle for moral, spiritual and legal rights as well as soap opera pregnant with speculative possibility.

There is much to be learned from the sisters. Read Genesis 29:32 through to Genesis 30:24 to see what the women name their sons and the one daughter. The names reflect the mother's state of mind. And for a fuller perspective on the anguished drama of the women and a sense of how humans strive for place and meaning, read the names of all the children of Leah and Rachel and their handmaids, Bilhah and Zilpah, with their Hebrew meanings.

Leah names her firstborn *Reuben; for she said, Surely the LORD hath looked upon my affliction; now therefore my husband will love me* (Genesis 29:32).

But Jacob does not.

Hoping after each of three births that now her husband will love her, after the birth of a fourth son, Leah, turning from what might be characterized either as an exclusive, obsessive desire for Jacob's love or a deep longing for knowledge of God, says, *"This time I will praise the LORD"* (Genesis 29:35 *NIV*). She calls the fourth child *Judah*. And it is *Judah* through whose line comes David, and Jesus.

And, the story tells us, children do not alone solve the problem of a loveless marriage.

Though loved to the hilt by her husband, Rachel is jealous of Leah's children and asks Jacob for children, *"or I shall die!"* (Genesis 30:1 *NRSV*). She echoes Rebekah's dramatic earlier statement. But Jacob, unlike his father, Isaac, who entreated the LORD on Rebekah's behalf, asks rather, *"Can I take the place of God?"* (Genesis 30:2 *NAB*). Here again is a reminder to consciousness about just who is husband and father. Jacob tells her to look not to an intermediary, even to him, her husband, but to God directly, *who hath withheld from thee the fruit of the womb* (Genesis 30:2).

She does.

Then God remembered Rachel; he listened to her and opened her womb. She became pregnant and gave birth to a son and said, "God has taken away my disgrace." She named him Joseph, and said, "May the LORD add to me another son."

(Genesis 30:22–24 *NIV*)

There is simply no question that the Bible says God is the Creator. The implications of this idea are profound and not always popular. But women who are having a hard time conceiving, women who want a child when it doesn't seem possible or probable, women who have a child by a less-than-wonderful-father may find it profitable to contemplate not only the lives of biblical women, but also the *Spirit of God* moving on the face of the *waters*. References to the words *remember, barren, fruit, womb* and *conceive* will be a helpful starting point for study.

Third and seventh days

Jacob had denied his own identity and deceived his own father in order to get Esau's birthright. And subsequently year after year, time after time, Jacob has been deceived by his father-in-law, Laban. Now Jacob has had it and no longer trusts Laban.

The Lord tells Jacob to go back to his own land. Jacob consults with Rachel and Leah (Genesis 31:3–15).

Earlier we read that the sisters were jealous of each other over their husband and children. We read now that when Rachel and Leah are consulted they are united. Jealousy seems to be something associated with an acute sense of a lack of power over one's own life. Consulted and united, with power over their own future, the sisters encourage Jacob to follow the Lord and support a move from their father's house.

> *"Surely all the wealth that God took away from our father belongs to us and our children. So do whatever God has told you."*
> (Genesis 31:16 *NIV*)

As they help move him into another state of consciousness as well as locale, Rachel steals her father's household gods. They all flee and it is *three days* before Laban discovers the group is gone, *seven* more before he overtakes them. The point here is probably not that Laban was preoccupied and that it took him three days to notice that more than half his household had left. The point here is to look instead to the *third* and *seventh* days.

Certainly the three-day lead time was helpful to Jacob and the women. But the *third day* may refer to spiritual Creation, where everything created is complete within itself (Genesis 1:11–13).

Perhaps in this reference to the *third day,* there is a sense that Laban, Jacob, Leah and Rachel — all those involved in this drama — are discovering that they are distinct, individual products of Spirit's Creation.

If one views the seven days that it took Laban to catch up with the group as referring to the *seventh day* of spiritual Creation, then the words that Laban hears from God put to rest the idea that there is anything at all to trouble Laban. And no reason for Laban to trouble Jacob (Genesis 31:24).

All are under Spirit's control.

If you find yourself in the midst of conflict, try dwelling instead in the sanctuary provided in biblical references to the *third* and *seventh* day. They will lead you to other references and force you out of turmoil and suffering into a pacific and timeless apprehension of your present experience.

There is another fine description of human nature when Laban finds the group and purports to be innocently wronged because Jacob went off without letting him say good-bye to his daughters and grandchildren. But what he really wants to know is why Jacob stole the household gods. The story is in Genesis 31:30–35, and you might enjoy reading and studying the story to learn more about how Rachel foils her father.

Israel

There is still a loose end, the brother Esau (Genesis 32; 33).

Jacob sends messengers to tell his brother that he hopes to make up. The messengers return saying that Esau met them with four hundred men. Jacob is greatly distressed by the news. He divides his people and possessions into two groups, thinking that if Esau kills one group, a remnant will be left.

Jacob prays to the God of his fathers, Abraham and Isaac, to be saved from Esau. Still cautious, Jacob sends gifts to appease Esau. In the middle of the night, Jacob takes his two wives, two handmaidens and his children — the members of his immediate family — leaves his campsite and then sends them all away.

And Jacob was left alone. (Genesis 32:24)

Here begins a seminal biblical story. That the man was alone is a reminder that each individual works out a relationship to God, alone.

And a man wrestled with him until the break of dawn.
(Genesis 32:24 *TNK*)

Earlier, Jacob's mother, Rebekah, has reported that Jacob had wrestled with his twin brother in the womb (Genesis 25:22), and Rachel says she wrestled with Leah (Genesis 30:8). *With great wrestlings have I wrestled with my sister, and I have prevailed* (Genesis 30:8).

Rachel's comment comes at the time of the birth of a child to Bilhah, her handmaid. And she names the child Naphtali, or "my strife." Jacob's wrestling will produce a nation.

And whoever Jacob is wrestling with — most likely himself — the *man* wants to be let go at the dawn of first *light*. But Jacob refuses to give up the struggle until he receives a blessing, this time won in truth, without duplicity, and in his own right — by individual struggle.

This wrestling with his own nature results in a new name, *Israel*. *For thou hast wrestled with God and with men and hast prevailed. ...And Jacob called the name of the place Peniel, for I have seen God face to face, and yet is my life reserved* (Genesis 32:28, 30 *Tyn*).

Jacob's name change to Israel is momentous. References to "Israel" are going to be more than references to one man. We are talking about a whole group of people from now on. A people — women and men — who, like Jacob, will bless and be blessed, deceive and be deceived, go astray and be led back, wrestle with themselves and with who they are until the moment they discover their real, their uncompromised, spiritual identity. "Children of Israel" is not only a reference to the descendants of Jacob but a metaphor for the person who goes through the struggle with self and recognizes God.

After the wrestling incident, Jacob and Esau are reconciled (Genesis 33), strange gods are put out of the family household (Genesis 35:1–4) and Rachel becomes pregnant again as she had foretold in Genesis 30:24.

Read these verses about Rachel in Genesis 35, in the *light* of what you already know about women in the Bible.

> *They set out from Bethel; but when they were still some distance short of Ephrath, Rachel was in childbirth, and she had hard labor. When her labor was at its hardest, the midwife said to her, "Have no fear, for it is another boy for you." But as she breathed her last— for she was dying— she named him Benoni; but his father called him Benjamin. Thus Rachel died. She was buried on the road to Ephrath— now Bethlehem.*
> (Genesis 35:16–19 *TNK*)

You know about *have no fear* or *fear not* — the first injunction given to women.

Some translations use the word *travail* for *labor*. *Travail* is the word used in conjunction with the woman in Revelation pursued by the great red dragon. Whether we read *travail* or *labor* doesn't change the essential female imagery. But the use of *travail* for "birth pains" means the contractions are not just localized, but generic to delivering an idea to earth — to human consciousness.

As her breath leaves her, Rachel names her child "son of my suffering" or "son of my strength," depending on how one translates *Ben-oni* (Genesis 35:18). The point here is that we should look at the words in the *light* of biblical themes concerning women. Even if we don't choose a meaning, we can assume the child was both the "son of her suffering" and the "son of her strength." Sometimes children seem a mixed blessing.

His father names him *Benjamin,* or "son of my right hand," or "son of prosperity," or "son of the south," which not only shows how different translations change a meaning, but that Rachel's choice of a name is overridden by her husband. Benjamin is to be an essential part of a later story. It is Benjamin's presence that ensures all the brothers acceptance into the plenty of Egypt in a time of scarcity for Israel (Genesis 44:26; 45:11–18).

You will see further that *son of my right hand* is a concept that traces clearly throughout the remainder of the Bible. We will see the significance of this seemingly small detail of translation when we read later what God says to Job (Job 40:14; see also Matthew 20:21, 23; Mark 16:19; Revelation 1:16, 17; 2:1; 5:1, 7). The study of the *right hand* as symbol is a volume in itself.

As we return to Rachel's story in Genesis 35:19, we read that Jacob buried Rachel *in the way of Ephrath, which is Bethlehem.* Rachel's dying in childbirth is not merely the end of one matriarch's story; it is the fertile ground from which another story of mother and child springs. For Bethlehem is where Mary will give birth to Jesus (Matthew 2:1; Luke 2:4–6).

Among the things being said here is that the lives of women in the Bible are connected and interwoven in birth, life and death and again birth. These stories connect not only the lives of individual women who are living with their God but, the Bible says, the lives of the people as a whole.

The prophet Jeremiah illustrates these associations: *Thus saith the LORD; A voice was heard in Ramah, lamentation, and bitter weeping; Rahel* [Rachel] *weeping for her children refused to be comforted for her children, because they were not* (Jeremiah 31:15).

Isn't Rachel one of our mothers? Don't we weep with Rachel

when we hear of innocents slaughtered over the vain pretensions of temporal political power?

The Bible repeats this theme prophesied by Jeremiah in many ways and in many places. The specific text is repeated when Mary takes the baby Jesus to Egypt for protection from Herod's order to kill all male children under two years of age (Matthew 2:16–18). You might want to reflect on the echoes of taking your child to Egypt for protection. You'll see clearly in the next story; in fact, by the end of the Book of Genesis, God takes the children of Israel to Egypt for their protection.

On the way to Egypt

The setup for the journey of Israel to Egypt is depicted through the story of Joseph, Rachel's eldest son. The story of his coat of many colors is familiar to almost all. Joseph is his father's favorite son. He tells his dreams before he has figured them out, and hatred and jealousy drive the ten sons of Leah, Bilhah and Zilpah to drop Joseph in a dry well. There is no *water* there. They mean for Joseph to die (Genesis 37:2–24).

But, while the brothers are eating *bread* (a possible hint toward communion), they *lift up* their eyes, moving the story into another dimension, and see some of Ishmael's descendants coming toward them on camels. Judah suggests that, instead of leaving Joseph to die in a dry well, the brothers should sell him into slavery (Genesis 37:25–36).

As in any respectable page-turner of a book, this chapter in the tale of the protagonist leaves Joseph in ambiguous circumstances. He is alive, but not free, in Egypt and in the house of the chief steward of Pharaoh.

Tamar

Let us interrupt our story of Joseph (as the Bible does) to look more closely into Joseph's brother Judah and to meet Tamar — one of the many biblical women who demand and receive their rights. Tamar's story is told in Genesis 38. Judah is the fourth son of Leah, the one whose name means "this time I will praise the Lord."

The story can be read as focused on Tamar — what she is entitled to and how she gets her entitlement. What we see here in the telling of Tamar's story is the continuing biblical evolution of consciousness that takes away the curse on Eve, and, too, a reversal of the idea that if a woman doesn't have children she is replaced by another woman. In Tamar's story it's the men who are replaced.

In six verses Judah leaves his brothers, marries, fathers three sons and chooses Tamar as wife for his firstborn son. That son dies and Judah tells his second son, Onan, to marry Tamar and *provide offspring* to his brother. But Onan, *knowing that the seed would not count as his, let it go to waste whenever he joined with his brother's wife, so as not to provide offspring for his brother* (Genesis 38:8–9 *TNK*).

And then Onan too dies and Judah tells Tamar to go to her father's house until his third son is grown and can marry her and give her the child or children to which she is entitled by law.

But Judah doesn't keep his promise to send the third son. Tamar does not feel sorry for herself. Nor does she carry on as if she were a victim. She takes action. Tamar puts off her widow's garments, covers herself with a veil, sits in an open place *by the way* and:

> *When Judah saw her, he took her for a harlot; for she had covered her face. So he turned aside to her by the road and said, "Here, let me sleep with you" — for he did not know that she was his daughter-in-law. "What," she asked, "will you pay for sleeping with me?" He replied, "I will send a kid from my flock." But she said, "You must leave a pledge until you have sent it." And he said, "What pledge shall I give you?" She replied, "Your seal and cord, and the staff which you carry." So he gave them to her and slept with her, and she conceived by him. Then she went on her way.* (Genesis 38:15–19 *TNK*)

Here's a familiar scenario: a woman claims her rights by placing herself on or in *the way*.

Judah does send a kid goat in exchange for his *seal, cord* and *staff* but no one can find (depending which translation you read) the *cult prostitute, whore* or *harlot* (Genesis 38:21). Further, all the men of the town say there was no harlot working that spot by the road.

About three months later, Judah hears that Tamar has *played the harlot* and that she is *with child by harlotry*. And Judah says to bring her to him. *"And let her be burned"* (Genesis 38:24 *TNK*). Here again we have hatred of the woman and her seed. How often have women and their children been destroyed by sexual accusation?

If you have been reading through Genesis and looked at the story

of Jacob's one daughter, Dinah, you will have seen the first biblical use of the word *harlot* (Genesis 34:31). There Dinah's brothers
provoke an early "international incident." Looking back a few chapters at Dinah's dilemma puts the accusation of Tamar as *playing the
harlot* in the context of male judgment. And, if you use your concordance to research the biblical use of the word *harlot,* you'll see
how the prophets use the word as a political term not reflective of
a spiritual state.

In the meantime, even though Judah must know he has denied
Tamar her rights, he would have her burned. This, from a leader of
one of the *twelve* tribes of Israel. Women today shocked at this type
of male behavior may also be shocked that it has gone on so long.

But when Tamar arrives at Judah's she sends him the symbols of
his authority — the *seal, cord* and *staff.* She says that she is pregnant
by the man who owns them. She has defended herself and put to
silence his self-righteous indignation (Genesis 38:25).

Stopped short, faced with the physical evidence, Judah reverses
his position and says that Tamar *"is more in the right than I"*(Genesis
38:26 *TNK*). She is not more righteous because of her actions, he
says, but by default. Judah did not keep his promise. He did not
send her the third son. Rather than waiting in line she was *on the
road, the way.* And she got her due from the head of the line. *And
he was not intimate with her again.* Judah has served his immediate
purpose in Tamar's life. Tamar's righteousness is obviously not of
the "goody two shoes" kind. She figures out how to get what she is
entitled to under the law and how — in advance — to protect herself
should she run into trouble with Judah later.

The ramifications of Tamar's story are manifold. Without her, the
name *Judah* (Juda in the New Testament) would not appear — as it
does — 823 times in the Bible. The name appears first as the son of
the mother who named him, then associated with the woman he has
selected first for his son. Then the name refers to the tribe of Judah,
then to his children, their children, the land and on into prophecy
and into the Book of Revelation.

Who is to judge?

Lot's daughters and Tamar, Sarah, Rebekah — and more biblical
women to come — take matters into their own hands. There is no
judgment on Lot's daughters, and Tamar is *more righteous* than the

head of the line of Judah. Later we will read Jesus' summation: *"If any one of you is without sin, let him be the first to throw a stone at her"* (John 8:7 *NIV*).

Whether one reads the Hebrew Bible or a Bible that includes the New Testament gospels, the texts make clear that the Bible and its God are on the side of powerless women. Some men may be for women and some may be against women. Women may have troubles with each other. No matter. The Bible, Spirit, God is on the side of powerless women.

Tamar gives birth to twins (Genesis 38:27), as did Rebekah. Through her out-of-wedlock encounter she is mother to the line of children who carry on through the male line to Boaz. Later in the Bible Ruth, a descendant of the incestuous relationship between the daughters of Lot and their father, marries Boaz. Ruth and Boaz are the great-grandparents of David the King. And we will see their names in the biological genealogy of Jesus (Matthew 1:1–16).

Joseph

Where Tamar's tale portrayed sex in the service of procreation, here the Bible cuts back to Joseph and his encounter with a woman who wants to seduce him, and procreation is not the issue. Joseph may be a dreamer, but he is trustworthy, and he rejects his master's wife's advances. Nevertheless his master throws Joseph into prison (Genesis 39:6–23).

Through many adventures Rachel's son Joseph makes his way through prison, where his ability to interpret dreams saves him and eventually places him second only to Pharaoh (Genesis 40; 41). In this position of power he gives grain to his brothers, whose father Israel (Jacob) has sent them *down to Egypt* when there is a famine in their own land (Genesis 42–45). Israel and his entire family join Joseph in Egypt (Genesis 46–47:28).

And the time drew nigh that Israel must die: and he called his son Joseph, and said unto him, If now I have found grace in thy sight, put, I pray thee, thy hand under my thigh, and deal kindly and truly with me; bury me not, I pray thee, in Egypt: But I will lie with my fathers, and thou shalt carry me out of Egypt, and bury me in their burying-place. And he said, I will do as thou hast said. (Genesis 47:29–30)

Israel's *twelve* sons are now the heads of the *twelve* tribes of Israel, and on his deathbed their father gathers them together and dissects their characters as he prophesies. It is an absolute *must* read (Genesis 49).

If you look at what Jacob says about each of his sons and remember what their mothers named them, you will see that the contrast is illuminating. Biblical names have meanings and carry allusions. They are meant to alert us to deeper significance and to connections between people. Joseph, for example, is portrayed here as a nice man, a good man, a man who serves others. Biblically speaking, we will see we are to take this background into consideration when we meet Joseph the husband of Mary and protector of her child, Jesus.

By looking at the differing perceptions of the heads of the *twelve* tribes, you should be able to judge human nature more effectively. And, of course, be alert to the biblical use of number *twelve* when you see it used again in the crown of *twelve* stars on the woman in Revelation 12:1. It's hard not to think of those *twelve* stars in her crown as reference to the brothers. And how do those *twelve* relate to the *twelve* princes descended from Ishmael?

Joseph is finally fully reconciled with his family. No hard feelings for his brothers' treachery. Joseph says it is God who has sent him ahead to Egypt. *"Besides, although you intended me harm, God intended it for good, so as to bring about the present result — the survival of many people."* (Genesis 50:20 *TNK*).

This is how the Israelites get to be in Egypt for 430 years; this sets the stage for Miriam, sister of Aaron, and her brother Moses, for the Passover and for the parting of the Sea, and for yet another return to the ideas of spiritual Creation described in the first chapter of Genesis.

Chapter Five

The Way Out

WHAT IF THE BIBLICAL GOD is not a dead concept but Being Itself easily recognizable not only in visions and by voice but by dramatic signs and physical healing? And what if you aren't exiled from this God who heals women?

The Book of Exodus is a study in the developing understanding of a Living, Present, All-Powerful, All-Wise, Saving Deity delivering not just one baby, one couple, or two, or *twelve* families, but a nation. The idea of God as a national and not just a personal Deliverer is developing. And again, it's not all sweetness and light. There is more labor and *travail* as well as triumph.

Spirit — that feminine, plural word for Creator — is very much present in Exodus. In fact, it's possible to see the first thirty-two verses of the chapter as not only an actual story but also as allegory reminding us, as we read, of *ruach Elohiym* and the *male and female* of Genesis 1:26–27.

The story of the Exodus of the children of Israel from Egypt begins with remembering as it repeats the names of the *twelve* sons of Israel who went to Egypt (Exodus 1:1). Much of Exodus is about remembering. Though no sketch can do Exodus justice, we will remember here some of the substance of the drama of Miriam, Moses, Aaron and the children of Israel.

Comes a Pharaoh who has forgotten Joseph (Exodus 1:8). This Pharaoh fears the increase in number of the Israelites after they've spent 430 years as guests in Egypt, and he enslaves them. But no matter how much they are oppressed, their birthrate continues to climb.

Pharaoh orders all male babies to be killed at birth. This attempt at ethnic cleansing — the consequence of an irrational fear of another people — will, after much tribulation, fail. The oppressed will be delivered. Exodus says that the process of deliverance from oppression begins with women. Shiphrah and Puah are midwives who blatantly disregard the instructions of their temporal ruler, Pharaoh, to kill male children.

> *The midwives, fearing God, did not do as the king of Egypt had told them; they let the boys live. So the king of Egypt summoned the midwives and said to them, "Why have you done this thing, letting the boys live?" The midwives said to Pharaoh, "Because the Hebrew women are not like the Egyptian women; they are vigorous. Before the midwife can come to them, they have given birth." And God dealt well with the midwives; and the people multiplied and increased greatly. And because the midwives feared God, He established households for them. Then Pharaoh charged all his people saying, "Every boy that is born you shall throw into the Nile, but let every girl live."*
>
> (Exodus 1:17–22 TNK)

Shiphrah and Puah obey, instead, their own individual consciousness of God. And they are rewarded with their own houses — a symbol, perhaps, that their consciousness of God provides "house." We are reminded again of the Twenty-third Psalm and the phrase *dwell in the house of the LORD forever.*

In a specific echoing of the Noah story, one of the Hebrew mothers makes an *ark* and puts her male baby in it (Exodus 2:1–10). Once more we are reminded that God saves. The baby's sister stands *afar off* to see what will happen next.

Pharaoh's daughter finds the baby in the *ark: She had compassion on him* (Exodus 2:6). Several things stand out here: *water,* women saving a child; the *ark* as a representation of safety; compassion unconfined by national or personal concerns.

The baby's sister says she knows a good nursemaid, her mother, the baby's mother. We will learn later that the mother's name is Jochebed (Exodus 6:20). The sister, mother and Pharaoh's daughter join together to save, nurture and support the child just as God is One and saves, nurtures and supports spiritual Creation — including the *male and female* of that Creation.

Once the child Moses is weaned, he will live in Pharaoh's house — under the nose of the one who has ordered the death of the boy child. It's as if the story says that God's child is not visible to evil and death.

It's easy to read in this Bible story that women from different cultures and religions negotiate together to save life. But when one reads this story as a specific, illustrative example of *ruach Elohiym*, of Spirit moving *on the face of the waters*, it makes perfect sense for Pharaoh's daughter to name the child Moses, *Because I drew him out of the water* (Exodus 2:10).

Here we are deep, deep in spiritual territory.

Look in your Bible at Chapter 2 of Exodus and count the references to *water*.

The *ark* is at the *river*.

Pharaoh's daughter has come to the *river* to *wash* herself; her maids are walking by the river's side; the baby *weeps*.

We will discover later that the name of the sister is *Miriam*, meaning "well" or "water." The Spirit of God that moved upon the *face of the waters* in Genesis 1:2 is moving still through Miriam. Even her name speaks *water*. And it is as if she reflects this Spirit as she watches the child being rescued by compassion — represented by Pharaoh's daughter. Even the name Moses (*because I drew him out of the waters*) alerts us that this story is about Spirit moving on *waters*. We will not be surprised later when the Sea parts and the people follow Miriam and Moses.

In less than a sentence after Pharaoh's daughter has named him, Moses appears as a grown man; and in the next sentence, he has killed an Egyptian he sees hitting a Hebrew (Exodus 2:11–15).

A mere five verses more and Moses has fled from Pharaoh, who wants him killed. Sitting by a *well*, he meets the seven shepherdess daughters of the priest of Midian. The women have come to draw *water* for their flock (Exodus 2:16).

Here again we are in the world of the literal and the world of symbol, reference and allusion. The flock, as we have read in Rachel's story, is often used biblically to represent not just sheep but numbers of people. The number seven is not only the sign of completeness represented by the seven days of Creation but also represents a blessing.

It is abundantly clear, by just the second chapter of the second book of the Bible, how densely layered the stories are. Once again the self-referential nature of the Bible can be clearly seen. The Bible's opening words are continually repeated in the lives of the characters. We are reminded of the spiritual Creation in Genesis in many ways — by numbers, names, elements.

Moses' encounter with the seven women at the well exemplifies a recurring biblical theme: how a man treats a woman has national and international repercussions through the ages.

The seven women are being harassed at the well by other shepherds who drive them away (Exodus 2:17–22). Moses rises to their defense and waters their flock. One verse, Exodus 2:17, is a description on a personal scale of what Moses will do later on a national scale. He will stand up to Pharaoh as he stands up to the shepherds, helping the Hebrews leave Egypt as he helps the seven daughters. And he will be with the women for forty years as the children of Israel will wander in the desert for forty years. The man Moses' experience with the seven women is extrapolated to the experience of the people and the nation as a whole.

But in the meantime the Bible describes daily existence. The father of the seven daughters asks them why they are home so early from work. They report that an Egyptian helped them. *Why is it that ye have left the man?* the women's father — who is a priest — asks (Exodus 2:20).

Entertaining strangers is biblical hospitality. *Call him, that he may eat bread. And Moses was content to dwell with the man: and he gave Moses Zipporah his daughter* (Exodus 2:20–21).

Does this mean Moses asked for Zipporah? Or that she asked for Moses? Is the only conclusion possible here that Zipporah exists solely as chattel? The Bible leaves these questions unresolved.

Much has been told in a short space. Further, before the end of the chapter God hears the groaning of the children of Israel and *God remembered the covenant with Abraham, with Isaac and with Jacob . . . and God had respect unto them* (Exodus 2:24–25).

The rest of the story — trouble and departure from Egypt, the continuing journey, the Ten Commandments and new definitions of God — will fill several books beginning with Exodus 3.

The burning bush

The biblical God supersedes the science that deals with matter and energy as motion and force. Moses is shepherding on Mount Horeb when *the angel of the LORD appeared unto him in a flame of fire out of the midst of a bush: and he looked, and, behold . . . the bush was not consumed* (Exodus 3:2). Isaiah 43:2; Psalm 104:4; Deuteronomy 4:33, 36; Acts 7:30–35; Hebrews 1:7; Revelation 1:14 and 19:12 are biblical passages that mention this *flame* and *fire*.

The flame of fire is magnified later as a *pillar of cloud by day*, [*and a*] *pillar of fire at night*, leading the children of Israel into the Promised Land. Look in Exodus 13:21–22 and 14:24 for some of the first references to this flame that leads *the way* for Moses' people.

Back again at Exodus 3:3, however, Moses is afraid to look at the bush or God.

The Lord sees that Moses turns aside. The text says that out of the midst of the burning bush God calls Moses by name: *Moses, Moses* (Exodus 3:4).

Moses replies: *Here am I*. Moses is describing his state of mind as well as his physical location.

The place whereon thou standest is holy ground, says God (Exodus 3:5).

The holy ground is not a building built with hands or machinery, not a center of social and political events, but, in this case, a patch of ground on a remote mountain. Moses didn't have to wait to die to go to heaven to experience holy ground. God is saying, wherever you stand may be holy ground; if you know who you are, it doesn't matter where you are.

Think of this when you are at the mall, in the laundry room, nursery, office. Where you are can be holy ground. You don't even have to be with people or like-minded people to stand on holy ground.

And we see in the account that, as in the story of Hagar, first an angel appears, then God. This progression may be the way you discover and experience God for yourself.

Moses hears from God that *I am the God of thy father, the God of Abraham, the God of Isaac, and the God of Jacob* (Exodus 3:6). Further, God has heard the cry of the Israelites and is sending Moses to lead them out of slavery, out of Egypt to a land flowing *with milk and honey* (Exodus 3:8).

Unlike Hagar, who simply names God, Moses wants to know the name of this God. The answer is not "Mysterious Unknown Big Man About to Punish You."

The answer is *Ehyeh-Asher-Ehyeh* (Exodus 3:14 *TNK*).

And here is another place, a central place in the revelation of God to human thought, where we need to pause and consider possible translations. As most biblical translators still are uncertain what the name means and some allow it may be that God can't be confined by name, there are different translations.

I Am That I Am. That's the King James, bold and firm.

"I am who I am" is another translation of *Ehyeh-Asher-Ehyeh,* found in the New Revised Standard Version, Good News Bible and the New International Version.

I will be what I will be, from the Tyndale, still another.

The answer Moses gets is still a source of reflection and exploration.

Hagar named God *El-roi* — a God who can be seen because, she said, *God sees me.* The response Moses gets from God is also in kind: It is how he responds to God's calling his name. *Here am I,* or *I am here,* Moses has said. This reflexive relation between women and men and God is ultimately without reference to time, space, gender.

I Am Who I Am tells Moses to tell Pharaoh, *The LORD God of the Hebrews hath met with us: and now let us go, we beseech thee, three days' journey into the wilderness, that we may sacrifice to the LORD our God* (Exodus 3:18).

By now the reader knows for sure that the *three days* is an allusion to the third day of Creation and that God is letting everyone know that things are moving into another dimension.

Provision

More good news comes with the reminder that God provides — *ye shall not go empty* (Exodus 3:21) — and that God's concern is inclusively about and for women:

> *"Each woman shall borrow from her neighbor, and the lodger in her house objects of silver and gold, and clothing, and you shall put these on your sons and daughters, thus stripping the Egyptians."* (Exodus 3:22 *TNK*)

The Hebrews need not leave empty-handed. Many today fear leaving the known for the unknown. From Abraham to Hagar to Rachel and Leah to the Israelites in Egypt, the Bible tells us that for every injunction to leave, there is a provision. No one must leave empty-handed.

The serpent and the rod

Although Moses accepts the messages, he fears that his people will not. He asks questions of God, who offers him proof to show the Hebrews in Exodus 4:2–4.

What is that in your hand?

A rod.

And the *rod* becomes a *serpent.* Moses grabs the *serpent* by the tail and it becomes a *rod* again. The *serpent* is illusion. Things are transformed into thoughts. This is information to take back to Eve in Eden. Read Genesis 3 again knowing as you do now from Exodus 4 that the *serpent* is an illusion — the opposite of the rod.

Turn again here to the Book of Revelation and read once more of the woman not only pursued by the *dragon* but about to give birth to a *man child who will rule with a rod of iron* (Revelation 12:3–5). Then the story of Moses, the *rod* and the *serpent* appears as not only a one-time event but in the context of biblical prophecy. The episode, cast in still another prophetic tone, is echoed in John 3:14:

And as Moses lifted up the serpent in the wilderness, even so must the Son of man be lifted up.

The serpent-to-rod-to-serpent is proof from God to Moses. The biblical God gives proof of Allness and spiritual power. The God of the Bible tells Moses to take the rod, *wherewith thou shalt do signs* (Exodus 4:17).

Power over flesh

In case the sign and power of the rod isn't enough, God tells Moses to put his hand in his *bosom.* Moses pulls it out covered with leprosy. He puts it back in his *bosom* and it is whole again — free of disease.

Most people want God to help them with the flesh, and the text has said that God has heard the people's cry. The I Am on Horeb has power over the flesh (as over conception earlier), evidenced when Moses puts his hand into his chest and first it is, and then it isn't, full of leprosy.

This chimerical phenomenon appears later on when Miriam (unfairly it seems to some) is struck with leprosy (Numbers 12:10). Moses, who was *very meek, above all the men which were upon the face of the earth* (Numbers 12:3), will ask, successfully, that the

Lord heal her. *Meek* is later a word central to the Beatitudes (Matthew 5:3–12), and Jesus' Sermon on the Mount draws from this characterization of Moses as meek.

The Bible is full of signs and healings — of acute changes of physical condition. Viewed not as miracle but as a natural part of spiritual Creation, healing is your right says the Bible. *I am the LORD that healeth thee,* says Exodus 15:26. Psalm 103:3 echoes this statement. It would be a mistake to trivialize or discount these references or to think that healing existed in biblical times only.

If you are looking for healing, looking for a God that is not abstract, a God that is immediate in your physical life, you may want to pick up your concordance and look for examples of healings. They can be a foundation for further study and reflection on your right to be healed, whole.

Passover

The story of the ten plagues visited upon Pharaoh who, no matter how much he may want to let the Israelites go, has his heart hardened by the Omnipresent Lord, is repeated each year in the celebration of Passover — a script of living drama, with an identification not just in the past but in the here and now. You'll find the story in Exodus 7:13 through Exodus 12:51.

Your heart will ache at the account. If you read the newspapers or watch television, you see striking similarities between the process of deliverance of the children of Israel and the situation now in many countries suffering famine, plagues and the death of young children. The Exodus story certainly addresses the consequence of personal and political actions as well as exemption from suffering.

The Passover meal contains certain elements with symbolic value including: *lamb* (Exodus 12:3); unleavened *bread,* a symbol of divine intervention (Exodus 12:8); bitter herb, an allusion to Exodus 1:14, *they made their lives bitter with hard bondage.* There are no instructions in this section of Exodus as to the gender of the person who leads the service at the meal. As you read the Passover drama for yourself, you will see the essential role women play in release from bondage. The Passover is referred to throughout the Bible, and in Matthew 26:17, Luke 22:7–20, Mark 14:12 and John 13:1 the meal is described or mentioned. Jesus' last Passover meal is referred to as the Last Supper.

Sea and land

Moses stretches his hand over the Sea, and the children of Israel walk on dry land. Moses and his people are fleeing from Egyptians and are plunging into the Sea — so it seems (Exodus 14:15–29). But spiritually speaking they are in the third day of creation. On the third day, the dry land appears, but only after the *waters* have been gathered together, as the seas have been gathered. Clock time and simultaneous time meet. The Sea parts. The dry land appears. The people live and are free. There are no oppressors left to follow them.

Woman's response

Now they must deal with God alone.
And here is how they begin to do that.
Miriam and all the women sing and dance.

> *Then Miriam the prophetess, Aaron's sister, took a tambourine in her hand, and all the women followed her, with tambourines and dancing. Miriam sang to them: "Sing to the LORD, for He is highly exalted. The horse and its rider he has hurled into the sea."* (Exodus 15:20–21 *NIV*)

Miriam's song will be echoed in part by Hannah, in 1 Samuel 2:1–11.

Ebbing and flowing

> *Then Moses caused Israel to set out from the Sea of Reeds. They went on into the wilderness of Shur; they traveled three days in the wilderness and found no water. They came to Marah, but they could not drink the water of Marah because it was bitter; that is why it was named Marah.* (Exodus 15:22–23 *TNK*)

In verses 22 and 23, just after Israel's passage through the Sea, Israel is also faced with the deprivation of three days with no *water*. Hard on the heels of joy is sorrow. A juxtaposition of joy and bitterness often reappears through the Bible as it does in life.

Moses cries out to the Lord, who shows him a piece of wood. Throwing the wood into the *water* changes the *water* from bitter to sweet. How this happens doesn't make much sense in the English. But looking to the Hebrew root for *wood* we find "to make firm;

hence to shut, especially the eyes." We remember that spiritual Creation described in Genesis 1:9–12 describes the gathering together
of the seas and then describes the fruit-bearing trees.

If all the root words and meanings are here given room, then
the story is not about a patriarch who is shown a two-by-four
piece of wood that somehow has miraculous, one-time power. It's
not impossible to allow that the people's eyes are opened to the
progression of days and abundant provision of Spirit's Creation.
Looking up the words takes about sixty seconds — and transforms
the story.

It's fairly clear to see here that it's a misconception to assume
the biblical Creator gives a blessing and then makes you endure a
hardship. Spirit blesses all. But opening the eyes to see the provision
of Creation is a prerequisite.

By chapter 19, the biblical idea of God is further developed in
new images: *You have seen what I did to the Egyptians, how I bore
you on eagle's wings and brought you to Me* (Exodus 19:4 *TNK*).

The foundation of God as both Mothering and Fathering has been
biblically laid from the Spirit *moving on the face of the waters* to the
protection of the Ark, to the I Am That I Am who is All-Being and
therefore The One Who Does All Things, and is Unlimited, Impossible to Confine and Presently Here. There is a nurturing and bonding
with the people seen in the image of God bearing Her children on
the wings of an eagle.

In this Mothering and Fathering, in this movement of protection
and definition of Eternal Consciousness, preparation is made for the
presentation of the Ten Commandments to the Lord's daughters and
sons.

The Ten Commandments

Some entertain the notion that the Commandments are a set of outdated prohibitions dropped down on stone by a vengeful, jealous
male God to His appointed male spokesman. But you know that
the Commandments come as part of a process of the revelation
of a Mothering and Fathering God. And look how they come to
consciousness.

*On the third day, as morning dawned, there was thunder, and
lightning, and a dense cloud upon the mountain, and a very*

*loud blast of the horn; and all the people who were in the camp
trembled.* (Exodus 19:16 *TNK*)

Attention must be paid.

*God spoke all these words, saying: I the LORD am your God who
brought you out of the land of Egypt, the house of bondage: You
shall have no other gods besides Me.* (Exodus 20:1 *TNK*)

All their experiences and a new understanding of the nurturing, caring, providing, ever-present nature of Spirit have led the
children of Israel to this point. This Me is no longer the tribal god
worshiped while in slavery. This *Me* is *Spirit* — the One Who Made
and Does All Things is beyond all representation in material form, is
not comparable to anything, anywhere, has provided rest, good and
completeness. The *I Am* is Sufficient. The *Tanakh* translates:

*You shall not make for yourself a sculptured image, or any like-
ness of what is in the heavens above, or on the earth below, or
in the waters under the earth.* (Exodus 20:4 *TNK*)

*You shall not swear falsely by the name of the LORD your
God.* . . . (Exodus 20:7 *TNK*)

Remember the sabbath day and keep it holy.
(Exodus 20:8 *TNK*)

*Honor your father and your mother, that you may long endure
on the land that the LORD your God is assigning to you.*
(Exodus 20:12 *TNK*)

In a literal sense the Commandments are the organizing princi-
ples of these people. Now these people are reminded to depend not
on the authority of a king or judge but on individual responsibility
to Deity, to the community and to the self.

"You shall not murder.
"You shall not commit adultery.
"You shall not steal.
"You shall not give false testimony against your neighbor.
*"You shall not covet your neighbor's house. You shall not
covet your neighbor's wife, or his manservant or maidservant,
his ox or donkey, or anything that belongs to your neighbor."*
(Exodus 20:13–17 *NIV*)

These Commandments are specific directives and certainly addressed to any mentality that feels there is not enough of everything to go around or that feels only anger, self-justification, lust, perjury and greed will provide.

Viewed not as prohibitions but as protection, the Commandments spare women and men the consequences of murder, theft, adultery, alert them to the ravages of envy and keep them from being assimilated in the land of "other" gods. Law, seated in individual behavior, protects both the individual and the community.

With the Commandments people can build homes and feel safe from theft. They can marry and not worry about sexual disease. They can work and play with their neighbors without looking over their shoulders in fear that they will be murdered. They can do these things if the Commandments are the law of the *seed* of Sarah/ Abraham — the Golden Rule of spiritual identity.

No one said it was easy to live the Commandments. It does take a certain meekness and concern for others. But it doesn't seem, from the way the world looks today, that it's much easier to live without them. Those who feel fettered by the Commandments might choose to view at them as protection — the way out of slavery.

Often the Commandments sound like thunder and lightning from a dense cloud. Sometimes what the Bible has to say does seem too much to bear in a single moment. And so, the Commandments are first simply presented and then they are commented on later. Certainly the Bible often demands a change of perception — to slow everything down, to work together for good, for balance. Living a quieter life goes hand in hand with an understanding of the Commandments.

Process upon process

The seemingly tedious, codified proscriptions that form the remainder of Exodus on to the end of Deuteronomy are offputting to many and the stuff of endless interpretation to others. Full of promise to powerless women, and with a God who includes both genders, the Bible still has its rough places. How women in varying traditions deal with these laws is a question of individual conscience and perception. Each individual stands in relation to her own concept of God and her own style of worship.

It may not cause your heart to burn within you to read Exodus

23:4–5, about an enemy's ass, which, prefiguration or not, may seem on the surface to have little relevance to today. On the other hand, Exodus 22:21–22 sounds like an immediate solution for contemporary political problems such as the status of refugees, health care and welfare reform.

Exodus 23 elaborates on the need to treat strangers well, on the Commandments, and it promises a cessation of sickness and a full-term completion of all pregnancies (Exodus 23:25–26). You may want to study the chapter for inspiration and a sense of promise.

When the first explication of the Commandments is over (there are others), Moses and Aaron and seventy-two others ascended *and they saw the God of Israel* (Exodus 24:10).

The glory

Moses went all the way *up into the mount,* and a *cloud covered the mount* and, in further commentary on the days of Creation outlined in the first chapter of Genesis, the Bible says:

> *And the glory of the LORD abode upon mount Sinai, and the cloud covered it six days: and the seventh day he called unto Moses out of the midst of the cloud.* (Exodus 24:16)

Here it is also worth pointing out a course you may wish to follow in your own study of the Bible. The *cloud* and *the glory* often illustrate the feminine, in-dwelling presence of God, or the Holy Spirit.

Following the *cloud* and the *glory* throughout the Bible leads to a fuller appreciation of how much of Scripture reflects the female aspect of Spirit. Following the promptings of this Spirit in the *cloud,* the *glory* and the *pillar of fire* leads to an intriguing line of research and revelation.

The remainder of the verses that describe Moses' experience are reiterations of all that has gone before. *Fire, children of Israel, forty days, days, nights, journey:* all symbols and signs and repeated reference to what has gone on and is now going on. There is one time here.

> *To the watching Israelites, the glory of Yahweh looked like a devouring fire on the mountain top. Moses went right into*

the cloud and went on up the mountain. Moses stayed on the
mountain for forty days and forty nights.
(Exodus 24:17–18 *NJB*)

This *glory* of the *cloud* is so real that the Israelites don't move on
their journey unless the cloud moves.

For Yahweh's cloud stayed over the Dwelling during the day-
time and there was fire inside the cloud at night, for the whole
House of Israel to see, at every stage of their journey.
(Exodus 40:38 *NJB*)

A reminder. Both the *glory* and the *cloud* are significant, recurring themes from Exodus to Revelation. Tracing them leads to *the*
way and beyond — to ultimate spiritual existence — waiting to be
seen and experienced without regard to denomination or personal
history.

Before he actually gets the children of Israel to the Promised
Land, Moses, who saw God *face to face,* dies in Moab. It is to be
Joshua who, filled with *the spirit of wisdom* (Deuteronomy 34:9 *NJB*)
brings the Israelites to *rest* and each to their own inheritance (Joshua
23:1, 4 *NJB*).

It is Joshua who says:

But if serving Yahweh seems a bad thing to you, today you must
make up your minds whom you do mean to serve, whether the
gods whom your ancestors served beyond the River, or the gods
of the Amorites in whose country you are now living. As regards
my family and me, we shall serve Yahweh. (Joshua 24:15)

Priestly duties

The third book of the Bible, Leviticus, is much about the spirit and
the letter of the law. Among other things, it contains a literal ren-
dering of a long list of priestly duties. Some of the things you will
find as you go through the pages of Leviticus: repeated references
to the *cloud* or *glory of the LORD,* God showing up in the details,
manna, what ages are appropriate for service, *serpents, rods, wells,*
and Moses emotionally at the edge, burdened by a complaining people who say they would rather have died in Egypt than trek through
the wilderness having to rely on God on a daily basis.

But no matter how much people complain, no matter what lengths they go to avoid God and their destiny, they are stuck with God. That's a concept that may well resonate with your life today.

The Book of Numbers helps us to see the constancy of God: *God is not a man, that he should lie; neither the son of man that he should repent* (Numbers 23:19).

By the time one has gone through Deuteronomy, one sees the Commandments repeated (people need at least more than one reminder, says the text); generosity and hospitality are the pre-requisites to *be perfect with the LORD thy God* (Deuteronomy 18:13).

There are references in these three chapters to caring for and saving women and children. Here too is demonstrated a high regard for marriage and woman:

> *When a man has taken a bride, he shall not go out with the army or be assigned to it for any purpose; he shall be exempt for one year for the sake of his household, to give happiness to the woman he has married.* (Deuteronomy 24:5 *TNK*)

There are rules and regulations for women who live in their father's or husband's houses, inheritance for women and a progressive understanding of God as unquenched, merciful, forever Love.

And there are places that seem to bring little comfort, that are disturbing or just plain confusing. In fact, there are not a few people who find the entire Bible as awkward as some of the *rough places.*

But as the Bible is aware of the tough places and demanding issues facing conscious thought, the Book speaks to the issue of rough places. Only one example is:

> *Every valley shall be exalted, and every mountain and hill shall be made low: and the crooked shall be made straight, and the rough places plain: And the glory of the LORD shall be revealed, and all flesh shall see it together: for the mouth of the LORD hath spoken it.* (Isaiah 40:4–5)

Valleys and crooked places are part of life and an adventure in the process of self-discovery.

Women, and the stories about women, can guide you through fields of despair and the tortuous complexities that sometimes appear along the way.

Chapter Six

Rough Places

HOW DO YOU GET THROUGH the rough places in the Bible? Let's take a look at a few examples.

There are places in the Bible where bad things happen to good or innocent people and places where the marginal and unnamed are treated badly. There are places that are so heavy with prescription and proscription that it's hard for the reader to tell at first glance what is going on. There are places that seem strikingly inconsistent. And there are those passages that seem dated, at best.

But, more often than not, the Bible tells how marginal and un-named people are treated better than kings and princes, and there are places so clear, so inspired, so familiar that they appear to be all the truth you have ever known.

There have been many explanations, many attempts at explana-tions of the rough places. Men and women have founded churches and formed denominations based on explanations of rough places as well as on their inspired vision of biblical texts. But whether or not the reader finds a satisfying explanation on the first, second or thou-sandth read (if that be the case) is up to the individual and the sense of revelation she has about the Scripture in front of her. Even that sense of revelation in a verse or story may take on more *light,* more focus as time glides by or as the eye and critical faculties become clearer.

Process and the tabernacle

The building of the tabernacle (Exodus 25 and on), while a favorite section for few readers, gives a glimpse into the methodology of some of the Bible and gives an indication of possible readings.

Not a few people through the ages have explained the copious instructions for the tabernacle as a symbolic description of the universe. To those readers, chapter 31 verse 3 of Exodus, *I have filled him with the spirit of God,* echoes the second verse of the first chapter of Genesis, *And the Spirit of God moved upon the face of the waters,* and is an indication that something is going on here that relates to Creation.

Others feel even today that these are the actual instructions for building a material sanctuary for the Lord. Others still think the instructions reflect the work it takes to develop a spiritual self. Aside from these constructions it is clear that the specific detail serves as a break so that consciousness does not dwell in nostalgia for the irreversible past or a desire to plunge into a fixed future.

The building of the portable tabernacle, which does not contain God, can be likened to reading the Bible. The Bible is portable, something quite remarkable that we now take for granted. And Deity may be found not only between the actual covers but in the very real process of searching, reading, meditating, acting on what is found there — in the weaving and joining and collecting and hammering down of disparate thoughts and ideas. In other words, as you read, study, put into practice what the Bible has to say to you, then you are building the tabernacle.

Instructions for building the tabernacle are given twice and broken up with a story in the middle: the building of the Golden Calf, which is a story of how not to and what not to build.

The first set of instructions for building the tabernacle begins when Moses comes down from his forty days and nights on the mountain. Amid the details of construction, it is stated in Exodus 35:5 that the tabernacle is to be built equally by men and women; who worked would be decided not by gender but by *whosoever is of a willing heart* (Exodus 35:5).

The women assembled at the door of the congregation as their mirrors were hammered down to make the laver in the center of the temple. Perhaps they are giving up a merely physical sense of beauty for a spiritual beauty. This passage may also indicate that a willingness to work on a project larger than oneself gives one a different identity.

The Golden Calf, the Tower of Babel, the Ark and Solomon's Temple are other things the Bible describes as being built. Some are at God's instructions, built for overall benefit; others, like Solomon's Temple, seem to be a trifle self-serving. Comparing each biblical construction might be of interest to someone building a house, to an architect, to anyone who is interested in learning how to read a story on more than one level or anyone interested in patience and the value of process in human life.

There is more to the seemingly tedious tabernacle section than first meets the eye.

Rape, dismemberment and murder

Certainly there are places in the Bible that many women today might find hopelessly out of date. What you think of these sections may have something to do with where you are today in your own conscious path of disentangling opinion from fact. Though there are options that might be considered as a point of departure, it is up to you to find explanations for some of these passages.

The Book of Judges is full of difficult, rough places. One reason it has been considered difficult may be because it illustrates that women are the movers and shakers of action and central to biblical events.

Taking a closer look at some of Judges illustrates possible approaches to rough places. In Judges are found most of the things that bother people about the Bible and about human life.

Judges illustrates violence and horrible behavior. Be alerted that the chronology doesn't always track in ways one might expect. And be warned again that there is violence, and violence against unnamed women. But it is not an apology for the Bible to say that there is no more or less violence within its pages than today on television or on the streets and roads of many cities and nations.

A glimpse of some of the texts shows that Judges itself says that not all may be sweetness and light:

> *In those days there was no king in Israel; every man did as he pleased.* (Judges 17:6 *TNK*)

The last verse of the book repeats this statement (Judges 21:25).

History and metaphor

Returning to the first six verses of the Book of Judges, there is a war led by Judah and seemingly encouraged by God, at least ten thousand people are killed, and Adonibezek loses his thumbs and big toes.

Anyone who thinks this is all in the gory, uncivilized past need only look at today's newspaper accounts of dismemberment and tribal and religious war.

But is the point here that nothing changes? Or does this account warn us, metaphorically, of the cutting apart, the fragmentation of the extremities of experience?

And what are we to make of the verse in Judges 1:12–15, where a woman given as a battle prize becomes one of numbers of women who get the good they ask for and more. Achsah, this particular woman, receives not only good but a blessing, as Jacob received a *blessing*, and not only land, but springs of *water*.

Women's history

Part of Judges, the story and song of Deborah, is thought by some to be the oldest biblical manuscript. Women's history has been with us as long as there has been history. How to interpret that history in the *light* of your experience can provide a clear highway for your journey through the Bible.

> *And she dwelt under the palm tree of Deborah between Ramah and Bethel in mount Ephraim: and the children of Israel came up to her for judgment.* (Judges 4:5)

Have you ever been told that as a woman you were too threatening? Check out Deborah. The prophetess Deborah has an entire nation and people at her disposal and the power of God to call men to her.

Biblically speaking, Deborah (also the name of Rebekah's nurse [Genesis 35:8]) sits under the tree that stands between Ramah and Bethlehem. Ramah is where Rachel weeps for her children; Bethel, where Jacob built an altar to the Spirit that renamed him Israel. There Deborah is — in the midst of the symbols of remembrance of both male and female.

Remembering that Deborah is part of a woman's heritage calls into question the notion that a female shouldn't serve in the armed forces. Deborah was commander-in-chief. Deborah reminds us that women lead in the name of the biblical God and that women can't be compartmentalized, marginalized or stereotyped.

Taking charge

And she sent and called Barak the son of Abinoam out of Kedesh-naphtali, and said unto him, Hath not the LORD God of Israel commanded, saying, Go and draw toward mount Tabor, and take with thee ten thousand men of the children of Naphtali and of the children of Zebulun?

And I will draw unto thee to the river Kishon Sisera, the captain of Jabin's army, with his chariots and his multitude; and I will deliver him into thine hand. (Judges 4:6–7)

What one makes of Barak's answer may depend on what one thinks of men. But there is no question he needs her.

But Barak said to her, "If you will go with me, I will go; if not, I will not go." "Very well, I will go with you," she answered. "However, there will be no glory for you in the course of the taking, for then the LORD will deliver Sisera into the hands of a woman." So Deborah went with Barak to Kedeh.

(Judges 4:8–9 *TNK*)

Did Barak know better than to go without Deborah? Or is a female leader a necessity for final victory?

The whole of Judges 5 is called Deborah's song. As you read that chapter, remember that it is characterized in female voice. Perhaps you want to read the whole song aloud to get the full import of woman's strength and place in prophecy, and in national and international events.

The villages were uninhabited in Israel, were uninhabited: until I Deborah arose, until I arose a mother in Israel.

(Judges 5:7 *Tyn*)

Fair self-assessment marks a biblical woman.

When phrases from Deborah's song reappear in the Psalms of David, the reader is reminded once more of the force and permanence of women's history.

Mimetic relationship is illustrated by Deborah's earlier prophecy that *the LORD will sell Sisera into the hands of a woman* (Judges 4:9), and the fulfillment of that prophecy when the woman, Jael, kills Sisera. The reader is painfully reminded, by the scene of Sisera's mother at the window, that for every victor there is a vanquished (Judges 5:28).

And after Deborah's victory and song, *the land had rest forty years* (Judges 5:31). Forty years is how long Moses stayed with his wife before the return to Egypt, how long the children of Israel wandered in the desert.

After the reign of a woman, *the land had rest for forty years.* Deborah is definitely a standard. Is there anyone who wouldn't want a woman for commander-in-chief if it meant that the land would have rest for forty years? A spiritual guide to life, the Bible certainly does not relegate women to proscribed positions.

Getting what you ask for

The story of Jephthah's daughter is certainly a rough place. It is one of those biblical accounts people point to when they say the Bible is anti-woman.

> *And Jephthah vowed a vow unto the LORD, and said, If thou shalt without fail deliver the children of Ammon into mine hands, Then it shall be, that whatsoever cometh forth of the doors of my house to meet me, when I return in peace from the children of Ammon, shall surely be the LORD's, and I will offer it up for a burnt offering.* (Judges 11:30–31)

Among other things, the story warns one to be careful about what is asked for and what is promised.

The grim result is that when Jephthah gets what he asks for, it is his only daughter who comes from his house, forcing him to change his mind or bring her to sacrifice. He doesn't change his mind. His concept of God is still locked in an outdated concept of Deity as rigid and requiring sacrifice.

> *And she said unto her father, Let this thing be done for me: let me alone two months, that I may go up and down upon the mountains, and bewail my virginity, I and my fellows. And he said, Go. And he sent her away for two months: and she went with her companions, and bewailed her virginity upon the mountains. And it came to pass at the end of two months, that she returned unto her father, who did with her according to his vow which he had vowed: and she knew no man. And it was a custom in Israel, That the daughters of Israel went yearly to lament the daughter of Jephthah the Gileadite four days in a year.* (Judges 11:37–40)

Not a very comforting story. Certainly a warning to make no foolish vows. And certainly a case of a woman and woman's seed being
attacked before bearing fruit.

The final verse of the chapter shows the need for women to
companion with other women and join in a ritual memorializing of
women by women. The four days that the *daughters of Israel* lament
are a significant reference to the feminine-gender fourth day of Creation in the first chapter of Genesis. And the lament may well be
for the attack on womanhood in the name of an outgrown sense of
what the biblical Lord requires.

The solidarity among women, in a time when *every man does that
which is right in his own eyes,* is plain. There is no reader who does
not know the feeling these women must have had. There is room
here for speculation that the story says all death is unfair, highlighted,
as the account is, by the daughter's innocence.

Fetal alcohol syndrome

Samson's mother (Judges 13:2–3) is a woman identified not by her
given name but by her relation to men. She is *wife, woman, mother.*
Her story, in some ways, is both specific and generic. It includes
words, phrases and actions found in the stories of Sarah, Abraham,
Isaac, Rebekah, Rachel, Jacob, Moses and Mary. And it twice includes a warning to a pregnant woman that is now on television
and liquor bottles: *"Now be careful not to drink wine or strong
drink..."* (Judges 13:4, 14 *NRSV*). That alcohol can damage the
fetus is knowledge that has been with the culture since the time of
Samson's mother.

The story also includes another instance of God controlling reproduction and God appearing first to a woman rather than a man,
and a woman offering logical and correct advice to a distraught man
(Judges 13).

Samson's own story (Judges 13–16) can easily be read as that of a
spoiled, demanding, promiscuous, foolish man. But there is no biblical judgment on whether he is good or bad. The story of Samson
is the stuff not only of opera but of the novel. It illustrates the en-
during nature of an old story that it is known at least in sketch form
even today — the long hair, the blinded eyes, the pulling down of
the temple.

In particular, the words of Delilah to Samson may sound familiar

to many modern readers. It's safe to say that some woman somewhere is asking her man the same question even now: *"How can
you say, 'I love you,' when you won't confide in me?"* (Judges 16:15
NIV).

Ending as the beginning

Toward the end of Judges is a story that echoes the dismembering
of Adonibezek in the opening of the book. There is a cutting up and
scattering abroad. As one looks at this tale one sees recurrent biblical
words and symbols. Beginning with *no king in Israel* there is reference to a *concubine* who played the *whore* (Judges 19:1–2). This
reference — as well as references to varying days on which activity takes place and to *straw* and *room to lodge in* (Judges 19:19) —
places the account in the realm of biblical faithfulness and hospitality
as well as in the domain of politics.

In this horrible story, a man who had been provided hospitality
forgets good in the face of fear of evil. He offers — as substitute
for a man who is his guest — his daughter (as did Lot) and wife/
concubine to *sons of Belial:*

> *... the man took his concubine, and brought her forth unto
> them; and they knew her, and abused her all the night until
> the morning: and when the day began to spring, they let her
> go.* (Judges 19:25)

There is no reporting of how the woman felt. When the Bible
wants us to know how people feel, the text tells us their feelings.
If emotions enter into this part of the biblical account, they are the
reader's and not the text's.

There are two things the reader might note about this scene.
One is that the female is seemingly valueless. But the other significant point here is that the father/husband/lover divides the abused
woman into twelve parts and sends her, like the tribes of Israel and
later like the twelve disciples, to all parts of Israel. If you do read
this story as literal, try also to read it as figurative and allegorical.
Certainly the female body is being spread throughout Israel.

The biblical comment on this story is:

> *And it was so, that all that saw it said, There was no such deed
> done nor seen from the day that the children of Israel came*

up out of the land of Egypt unto this day: consider of it, take
advice, and speak your minds. (Judges 19:30)

Paradox

The last story in the Book of Judges is about the capture of four hundred nameless virgins from Shiloh (Judges 21:12). In typical biblical
paradox, it prefaces a series of stories that we will look at through the
next several chapters that laud, praise, celebrate and honor specific,
named, independent women.

Looking closely at Judges, it's possible to say that the rough
places aren't so rough after all. Rough places are descriptive, horren-
dous, allegorical and instructive. Equally they are warnings, advice,
figurations and prefigurations as plain as the advice not to cross the
street against the light nor touch a hot stove with your bare hand.

Chapter Seven

Plain Places

WHAT IF IT WERE POSSIBLE to show our daughters, nieces, students, friends, sisters, aunts and mothers that the Bible — without regard to age or physical endowments — was full of good for women? What if we are the first full generation of women who say, once and for all, that the biblical God loves women as Her full idea, cherishes women, understands women and helps women wherever they are?

Let's start this process by remembering what the biblical God has done for women so far in just six books of the Bible:

- Created women as the highest idea of generic man.

- Illustrated the dangers of domination of women.

- Showed that there are no limits to conception.

- Sent angels to powerless, fearful women.

- Appeared to women's eyes.

- Saved women's children.

- Given women husbands who love them.

- Provided homes for women.

- Protected women.

- Healed women of physical ills.

- Approved women's strength and leadership abilities.

- Anointed women as leaders.

- Made women rulers over their own bodies and minds.

- Given women occasion to sing and dance.

- Said women work equally with men.

- Anointed women to carry the message of God to all.

- Exempted women from criticism on sexual, domestic and political actions.

These are the simply obvious things.

Aware, inspired by the biblical God's creation of us as the apex of Creation in an ordered universe — and a dimension beyond even the universe — what woman would want a limited, stultifying life of suffering and punishment?

Who would be Eve?

Chapter Eight

The Woman Alone

What if the Bible said that the widow, the orphan, the powerless woman carry the story of God to earth? What if being a woman alone isn't a dead-end street but an open way to happiness, fulfillment and self-esteem?

Let's take a look at the women in Ruth and on into the First Book of Samuel and see that not only does God provide for the woman alone but that without seemingly powerless women there would be no story of God's provision for earth. No completeness and no happy ending.

Faithful or smart?

The familiar *whither thou goest, I will go; and where thou lodgest, I will lodge: thy people shall be my people, and thy God my God* (Ruth 1:16) is Ruth's line. Many think that a woman says that to a man, but in fact Ruth says it to her mother-in-law, Naomi. These phrases have been associated with the marriage ceremony and, in the past, have often been used to relegate both Ruth and Naomi to non-threatening, stereotypical roles by casting them as devoted daughter-in-law and helpless widowed women.

Guess again. Ruth and Naomi are not one-dimensional figures. They are smart women making smart choices. They seem powerless but are protected, guided, nurtured, elevated, and they know themselves as they clearly, oh so clearly, assess their options in a sexist world. They represent the superseding of a hopeless condition by spiritual sense. They illustrate a narrative of spiritual power for women.

Bitter and Sweet

The four chapters of Ruth tell the story of how women alone make it in the world and how it happened that David came to earth. These four chapters are breathtaking in their simplicity and allusion. Sections like this make the Bible the Book it is. After all, we seek in its pages inspiration, not mere information.

In just four chapters the women are widowed, made outcasts in the land, return to Naomi's original home, find housing, employment and the protection of the most powerful man in the community and produce an heir to be remembered forever. Not bad work for two women in any time or place.

Start reading Ruth and you will see again that the story starts out with men and then, in a few verses, when things actually start happening, switches to women. Naomi is the central figure.

> *Then she arose with her daughters-in-law, that she might return from the country of Moab: for she had heard in the country of Moab how that the LORD had visited his people in giving them bread.* (Ruth 1:6)

As Abraham did, Naomi gets up and goes. But Abraham did not move until he got a direct order from God. Naomi acts solely on something she has heard.

Few things in the Bible are more glorious than the sight of women finding their own way against all odds. Orpah finds hers when she returns to her people, and Ruth and Naomi find theirs when they return to Bethlehem in the *barley harvest*. The signification is clear. In pastoral times where would you be but at home in the midst of plenty? Harvest time is not just a time of year but symbolic of *abundance* both material and spiritual.

Naomi is a marvelous character. When she re-enters Bethlehem (meaning "house of bread") after years of exile in Moab with a husband and sons, she says: *Call me not Naomi, call me Mara: for the Almighty hath dealt very bitterly with me* (Ruth 1:20).

This a specific allusion (known to all the townspeople who listen) to the women who left Egypt with Miriam and Moses and Aaron and found bitter (Marah) *waters*. Here is a biblical woman who is not afraid to call attention to her problems. Many things can be learned from Naomi. She had faith that the Lord was providing. But still she let everyone know that her life had not been uneventful.

You may feel the same way. You may feel the Lord is caring for you but that you have also gotten the short end of the stick. But through this ebbing and flowing stage of consciousness, Naomi is cared for. Ruth asks permission *to go to the field, and glean ears of corn after him in whose sight I shall find grace* (Ruth 2:2). The field belongs to Boaz, who by Hebrew law is in the line of men who owe the women protection.

Wings in the wilderness

Ruth, like Sarah and Abraham, has left her family. And she is rewarded. *The LORD recompense thy work, and a full reward be given thee of the LORD God of Israel, under whose wings thou art come to trust* (Ruth 2:12), Boaz says to Ruth. Those wings again, as in Exodus, bringing the children of Israel and in this case a daughter of Moab under the protection of the nurturing God.

Each verse of this story should be examined by women who feel alienated, adrift, hungry, unloved, as well as by women and men who think that they are planning their own futures.

Take a look at the barley harvest. It says much for women that needs to be said. It meets the human need. Look up *fruit, harvest* in your concordance and see if those words lead you to a sense of fulfillment.

As inspiration, Ruth and Naomi live forever in poetry and history. They are also the great-grandmother and great-great-grandmother of David, the psalmist, unifier of Israel, lover of many women and central to the line of prophecy. Ruth, David's great-grandmother, is a Moabitess, a descendant of Lot and his daughter. Boaz, who will father a child by Ruth, is a descendant of Tamar (who *played the harlot* to ensure her rights in the face of her forgetful father-in-law, Judah).

The initiative of these women — Lot's daughters on the female side and Tamar on the male side — bring the biological David into the world. And it is David who unifies Israel by accepting the foreigners and strangers. When we remember that his great-grandmother was a foreigner and stranger in Bethlehem and we remember how many of us have learned from our ancestors, we see again the importance of women in shaping the course of history.

One reads on from the Book of Ruth without interruption to the First Book of Samuel and to Hannah, whose story, like Ruth's, begins with a man who fades into the landscape of the desires and needs of women. There is no question that in these chapters the Bible is unfolding its story through women.

Knowing and desire

Hannah is a key biblical figure. Not only does she share with Rachel the provocations of another wife, not only is she the most beloved, she establishes silent prayer (1 Samuel 1:2–10).

Certainly it is not because she is loved or that she envies and is provoked that her name lives today as one of the seven women prophets of Israel. She lives on because of how she prayed, her specificity, her sense of certainty about her own individual relationship, rights and access to the Lord and her song.

Look at Hannah's prayer from verse 11 of the first chapter. Note the same bitterness that the women encountered after the parting of the seas, the same bitterness Naomi spoke of earlier.

Follow along with Hannah and note how specific she is.

> *And she vowed a vow, and said, O LORD of hosts, if thou wilt indeed look on the affliction of thine handmaid, and remember me, and not forget thine handmaid, but wilt give unto thine handmaid a man child, then I will give him unto the LORD all the days of his life, and there shall no razor come upon his head.* (1 Samuel 1:11)

Not cutting your hair is a sign of devotion to God.

Then Hannah talks back to a priest. The reader will note that when Hannah is misrepresented by the priest and talks back to him, she is not censured, ostracized or cast out of organized religion.

> *And Eli said unto her, How long wilt thou be drunken? put away thy wine from thee. And Hannah answered and said, No, my lord, I am a woman of a sorrowful spirit: I have drunk neither wine nor strong drink, but have poured out my soul before the LORD. Count not thine handmaid for a daughter of Belial: for out of the abundance of my complaint and grief have I spoken hitherto.* (1 Samuel 1:14–16)

Belial represents those drunken louts who have their way with the concubine/wife in the Book of Judges, and Hannah knows she has nothing to do with that kind of behavior. She uses the word *abundance,* the name of Sarah, the mandate of Genesis 1:20 — let life be brought forth *abundantly.* This is not a mere petition for a child. Hannah places herself in spiritual Creation with the reference to the word *abundant.*

The priest gives up. He yields to the woman and her more enlightened concept of Creation. After the fact he gives the priestly blessing: *Then Eli answered and said, Go in peace: and the God of Israel grant thee thy petition that thou hast asked of him* (1 Samuel 1:17).

Hannah and her husband worship before the Lord and return home, and ...*Elkanah knew Hannah his wife; and the LORD remembered her* (1 Samuel 1:19).

Here is one of countless places in the Bible where the text illustrates the side-by-side creations of Genesis, chapters 1 and 2. Elkanah, like Adam, *knew* his wife. But, *the LORD remembered* Hannah, as God remembered Noah, as Rachel was *remembered.*

Hannah's first child, Samuel, will anoint David, great-grandson of Ruth, great-great-grandson of Naomi, as king of Israel. The line of women is unmistakable not just biologically but in the anointing, prophesying, praying, acting, being, doing, living with the Creative Spirit of the Bible.

Hannah had prayed silently for this child, and after his birth she prayed aloud. Her prayer was not a sweet "thank you," but as we read in 1 Samuel 2:

> *"My heart rejoices in the LORD,*
> *in the LORD my horn is lifted high.*
> *My mouth boasts over my enemies,*
> *for I delight in your deliverance.*
>
> *There is no one holy like the LORD;*
> *there is no one besides you;*
> *there is no Rock like our God.* (1 Samuel 2:1–2)

Read on where Hannah says,

> *The bows of the warriors are broken,*
> *but those who stumbled are armed with strength.*
> . . . .
> *She who was barren has borne seven children,*
> *but she who has had many sons pines away.*

The LORD brings death and makes alive.

. . . .

For the foundations of the earth are the LORD's;

. . . .

those who oppose the LORD will be shattered.
He will thunder against them from heaven;
the LORD will judge the ends of the earth.

He will give strength to his king
and exalt the horn of his anointed.

(1 Samuel 2:4, 5–6, 8, 10–11 *NIV*)

This is not tame stuff. Nor is it bragging. It is prophecy spilling out of the mouth of a biblical mother. Mary repeats part of Hannah's song when she receives the knowledge she will bear a child through God alone. Women through the ages are connected to each other, live and move and have their being in God as well as in each other's hopes and aspirations.

Chapter Nine

Bundles of Life

WHAT IF THE BIBLE SAYS your own prophetic ability can get you out of a bad marriage?

Let's look at Abigail, who, in less than two weeks, goes from being cast as a lovely but unknown woman of great wisdom married to a foolish drunk to being a prophet, married instead to a gracious, passionate, warrior poet, the Lord's anointed and the king of Israel.

Although we most often hear about David and Bathsheba or about David and Saul's daughter, Michal, nevertheless the story of David and women is at its high point with Abigail — neither a seducer nor the seduced nor the daughter of a powerful man. Abigail is another of the seven women prophets of Israel, a most political woman, and by almost any definition one of the smartest. There is much to be learned from Abigail.

Enter Abigail

David's victory over Goliath is past (. . . *who is this uncircumcised Philistine, that he should defy the armies of the living God?* [1 Samuel 17:26]). David has married Michal, one of King Saul's daughters, survived Saul's love, and then jealousy and repeated attacks; taken refuge for a time in Ramah with Hannah's son, the Lord's prophet Samuel. Now, just after Samuel's death, David is grieving and

> . . . *David arose, and went down to the wilderness of Paran. And there was a man in Maon, whose possessions were in Carmel; and the man was very great, and he had three thousand sheep, and a thousand goats: and he was shearing his sheep in Carmel. Now the name of the man was Nabal; and the name of his wife Abigail: and she was a woman of good understanding, and of a beautiful countenance: but the man*

was churlish and evil in his doings; and he was of the house of Caleb. (1 Samuel 25:1–3)

Here again the Bible begins a story about men and then switches to the story of a woman. And, here again, the story shows that how men and women treat each other has national and international repercussions through time.

The story continues as David sends ten of his men over to Carmel to greet Nabal in David's name and request hospitality; *bread, water* and *lamb.* On your trip through the Bible so far you've already seen that hospitality is the number one prerequisite for entertaining angels and God and, in a more general sense, for making your way through the wilderness of human hope.

Remember that Abraham (Genesis 18) exhibits hospitality to the three men who announce that Sarah will conceive, and, in one of the 129 biblical references to the word *stranger,* the Lord tells the children of Israel: *Thou shalt neither vex a stranger, nor oppress him: for ye were strangers in the land of Egypt. Ye shall not afflict any widow, or fatherless child. If thou afflict them in any wise, and they cry at all unto me, I will surely hear their cry* (Exodus 22:21–23).

It's a mandate.

And yet Nabal refuses hospitality, saying he's never even heard of this David and wonders if perhaps he is just a runaway servant. David — macho to the hilt — girds up his sword at this response and takes four hundred armed men with him in a plan to attack Nabal. Readers will note that four hundred armed warriors is the same number that Jacob was told accompanied Esau. No loose ends in biblical accounts of men arming themselves to settle personal disputes.

> One of the servants told Nabal's wife Abigail: "David sent messengers from the desert to give our master his greetings, but he hurled insults at them. Yet these men were very good to us. They did not mistreat us, and the whole time we were out in the fields near them nothing was missing. . . .
>
> "Now think it over and see what you can do, because disaster is hanging over our master and his whole household. He is such a wicked man that no one can talk to him."
>
> (1 Samuel 25:14–15, 17 *NIV*)

You can see that biblical men ask women what they think should be done and expect them to take care of things.

Abigail doesn't pause for an instant. She doesn't defend her husband. Nor does she run and tell her friends or her mother or her co-workers that she married a horrible man who is disgracing her and might even get her killed.

She takes matters into her own hands — immediately.

Abigail lost no time. She took two hundred loaves of bread, two skins of wine, five dressed sheep, five seahs of roasted grain, a hundred cakes of raisins and two hundred cakes of pressed figs, and loaded them on donkeys.

Then she told her servants, "Go on ahead; I'll follow you." But she did not tell her husband Nabal. As she came riding her donkey into a mountain ravine, there were David and his men descending toward her, and she met them.

(1 Samuel 25:18–20 *NIV*)

Not only does this look like a great picnic, not only does Abigail not tell her husband, she has quite clearly moved into the land of spiritual territory and prophecy.

I'll follow you is translated by the King James Version as *behold, I come after you* and is reminiscent of what John the Baptist says (Matthew 3:11). Riding on a donkey is not just a method of transportation in Abigail's day. The animal represents an announcement of protection or things to come. Among other donkey riders, Moses led Zipporah and her children into Egypt, later Joseph will lead Mary and her child on the way to Egypt and lastly Jesus rides a donkey as palms are thrown before him.

Abigail is on her way to intercept a furious David — a David boiling over with self-righteous male indignation.

Now David had said, Surely in vain have I kept all that this fellow hath in the wilderness, so that nothing was missed of all that pertained unto him: and he hath requited me evil for good. So and more also do God unto the enemies of David, if I leave of all that pertain to him by the morning light any that pisseth against the wall. (1 Samuel 25:21–22)

That's about as macho as it gets.

But when Abigail sees David, she gets off the ass and falls to the ground in front of his feet. Whether you think it is groveling, the opening of a very clever piece of politics or actions in the line of prophecy, here is what she says:

Upon me, my lord, upon me let this iniquity be: and let thine handmaid, I pray thee, speak in thine audience, and hear the words of thine handmaid. Let not my lord, I pray thee, regard this man of Belial, even Nabal: for as his name is, so is he; Nabal is his name, and folly is with him: but I thine handmaid saw not the young men of my lord, whom thou didst send.

(1 Samuel 25:24–25)

And whether you think she has just trashed her husband, told the truth about him or ended slaughter and war before it started, may cause you to examine your own understanding of a woman's response to a dangerous situation.

And whether you think what Abigail says next makes her a flatterer or a model of diplomacy and a candidate for Secretary of State may cause you further to examine your own feelings about women, women's intelligence and women's role in politics and the affairs of the nation.

Turning to a tight and intricate reference to David and the Lord, she prophesies. Look very closely in your Bible at how she calls David *lord* in the very same breath that she acknowledges the LORD as the living God. Look at how she says that only the LORD is more powerful than David (even though she is quite powerful as she interrupts David on his way to murder her husband). She may recognize herself as the LORD's instrument in David's life, but what she says is:

Now therefore, my lord, as the LORD liveth, and as thy soul liveth, seeing the LORD hath withholden thee from coming to shed blood, and from avenging thyself with thine own hand, now let thine enemies, and they that seek evil to my lord, be as Nabal.

And now this blessing which thine handmaid hath brought unto my lord, let it even be given unto the young men that follow my lord.

I pray thee, forgive the trespass of thine handmaid: for the LORD will certainly make my lord a sure house; because my lord fighteth the battles of the LORD, and evil hath not been found in thee all thy days.

Yet a man is risen to pursue thee, and to seek thy soul: but the soul of my lord shall be bound in the bundle of life with the LORD thy God; and the souls of thine enemies, them shall he sling out, as out of the middle of a sling. (1 Samuel 25:26–29)

Biblical women know how to use language, and she sees it. She sees David *bound in the bundle of life with the LORD thy God.*

Miriam's Song, Deborah's, Hannah's, all carry much wisdom, strength and prophecy. Abigail uses an alert reference to the sling, which David used to slay Goliath, a reference David knows only too well. Learning from Abigail we might well learn how to pull out a handy fact to serve our and God's purposes. Abigail then ties together a reminder to David that he, David, is to be king, warning that an attack on Nabal will be disastrous to his future.

And it shall come to pass, when the LORD shall have done to my lord according to all the good that he hath spoken concerning thee, and shall have appointed thee ruler over Israel; That this shall be no grief unto thee, nor offence of heart unto my lord, either that thou hast shed blood causeless, or that my lord hath avenged himself: but when the LORD shall have dealt well with my lord, then remember thine handmaid. (1 Samuel 25:30–31)

Abigail ensures a place for herself in the *bundle of life.* She will occupy an equal place — bound in the *bundle of life.*

Abigail ties David to God, God to David and herself to both of them. Along with Abigail, you too can see beyond the immediate situation and, along with Abigail, share in women's prophetic vision — being bound in the *bundle of life.*

See then how David treats Abigail and see why David was loved by women. See if what he says and the way he says it isn't something you'd like any man in your life to say to you:

And David said to Abigail, Blessed be the LORD God of Israel, which sent thee this day to meet me: And blessed be thy advice, and blessed be thou, which hast kept me this day from coming to shed blood, and from avenging myself with mine own hand. For in very deed, as the LORD God of Israel liveth, which hath kept me back from hurting thee, except thou hadst hasted and come to meet me, surely there had not been left unto Nabal by the morning light any that pisseth against the wall.

(1 Samuel 25:32–34)

Now the man David puts God, not himself first. David acknowledges that Abigail is acting for God. He puts her advice in the category of the sixth and seventh days of spiritual Creation by calling it *blessed.* And not only does he think her advice is beyond all human

advice; he specifically acknowledges her actions. It would be hard
not to love a man who appreciated you the way David appreciates
Abigail. He says, *Go up in peace to thine house; see, I have hearkened
to thy voice, and have accepted thy person* (1 Samuel 25:35). David
accepts not merely Abigail's evidences of hospitality, not merely her
words, not only her deeds. He gives the most important acceptance
of all, the acceptance of her as a person.

The story comes to poetic fulfillment without missing a beat.

Abigail goes home to find Nabal drunk and stuffing himself with
food. In the morning, when he is sober, Abigail tells him what went
on between her and David. At the news Nabal has a heart attack.
Ten days later he dies.

> *Then David sent word to Abigail, asking her to become his wife.*
> (1 Samuel 25:39 *NIV*)

Not only is there no traditional mourning period here; they must
have had a great time communing, and she must have said "yes"
because David sends his servants to her house *to take [her] to him
to wife* (1 Samuel 25:40).

We are conditioned today to have a respectable mourning period
after a spouse's death and to be careful that we don't marry out of
some codependent or psychotic need. Whatever the source of those
concerns they are not the Bible's at this point.

And in another example of how women pave the biblical way,
Abigail washes the feet of David's servants, as Jesus will later do for
his disciples, the servants to the early church.

> *Behold, let thine handmaid be a servant to wash the feet of the
> servants of my lord. And Abigail hasted, and arose, and rode
> upon an ass, with five damsels of hers that went after her; and
> she went after the messengers of David, and became his wife.*
> (1 Samuel 25:41–42)

Abigail's story doesn't end there. She is captured by enemies of
David, is rescued by him, and bears him a child; she is yet another
biblical woman whose experience is full of adventure.

There is no question that the women who came into contact
with David have their share of adventure, danger, drama and triumph. A partial list of women who have encounters with David
includes Michal, Bathsheba, Abigail, Abishag, women like Rizpah

(whose sons died in David's reign), two Tamars (his daughter and a granddaughter), Ahinoam and Zeruiah, his half-sister.

In his time, there are also *wise* women, the witch at Endor (1 Samuel 28:7–25), the women widowed and left fatherless by David's battles as he unified Israel. The list of women influenced and affected by David even after his death (recorded in 1 Kings 2:10) is a long one and interesting in that it illustrates clearly a variety of women and of female experience.

And the women? How did they influence David? Did David write down all those wonderful Psalms — full of ideas that feed the heart of women starving for spiritual comfort — as they fell from the lips of Abigail, Bathsheba, Michal or Abishag?

Chapter Ten

Psalms

FEMALE EXPERIENCE — all experience — is enriched by the Psalms. Written at different times under different circumstances, the Psalms are prophetic, personal and impersonal, individual, national, reflective, timely and, to some, boastful. The Twenty-third Psalm, which begins, *The LORD is my shepherd,* and the Ninety-first, *He that dwelleth in the secret place of the most High shall abide under the shadow of the Almighty,* are familiar comforts to many. Jesus repeats part of the prophetic Psalm 22 on the cross (Matthew 27:46).

In some ways, Psalms can be read as an overview of the Bible. Some, like Psalm 22, look ahead to Jesus and the New Testament. Other psalms go back into parts of the Bible we have already read. Psalm 106 recaps the story of Moses and the children of Israel led out of Egypt. Psalm 104 comments on spiritual Creation, as does Psalm 148.

Whether many scribes had a hand in the Psalms, or whether David wrote some of those attributed to him while in the presence of Abigail, Bathsheba, Michal, Abishag (or any of the women who made his life the richer) is of less importance than the fact that the reader today can search through them with the knowledge that the author lived a full life, loved women and speaks out of experience. No one can deny that the Book of Psalms is gorgeous.

Here are some passages that may speak to you today.

O ye sons of men, how long will ye turn my glory into shame? how long will ye love vanity, and seek after leasing?

(Psalm 4:2)

I will both lay me down in peace, and sleep: for thou, LORD, only makest me dwell in safety.

(Psalm 4:8)

My voice shalt thou hear in the morning, O LORD; in the morning will I direct my prayer unto thee, and will look up.

For thou art not a God that hath pleasure in wickedness: neither shall evil dwell with thee.

(Psalm 5:3–4)

Lead me, O LORD, in thy righteousness because of mine enemies; make thy way straight before my face.

(Psalm 5:8)

Depart from me, all ye workers of iniquity; for the LORD hath heard the voice of my weeping.

The LORD hath heard my supplication; the LORD will receive my prayer.

Let all mine enemies be ashamed and sore vexed: let them return and be ashamed suddenly.

(Psalm 6:8–10)

When I consider thy heavens, the work of thy fingers, the moon and the stars, which thou hast ordained;

What is man, that thou art mindful of him? and the son of man, that thou visitest him?

For thou hast made him a little lower than the angels, and hast crowned him with glory and honour.

Thou madest him to have dominion over the works of thy hands; thou hast put all things under his feet:

All sheep and oxen, yea, and the beasts of the field;

The fowl of the air, and the fish of the sea, and whatsoever passeth through the paths of the seas.

O LORD our Lord, how excellent is thy name in all the earth!

(Psalm 8:3–9)

LORD, thou hast heard the desire of the humble: thou wilt prepare their heart, thou wilt cause thine ear to hear:

To judge the fatherless and the oppressed, that the man of the earth may no more oppress.

(Psalm 10:17–18)

Keep me as the apple of thy eye, hide me under the shadow of thy wings.

(Psalm 17:8)

The heavens declare the glory of God; and the firmament sheweth his handiwork.

Day unto day uttereth speech, and night unto night sheweth knowledge.

There is no speech nor language, where their voice is not heard.

Their line is gone out through all the earth, and their words to the end of the world. In them hath he set a tabernacle for the sun,

Which is as a bridegroom coming out of his chamber, and rejoiceth as a strong man to run a race.

(Psalm 19:1–5)

But thou art he that took me out of the womb: thou didst make me hope when I was upon my mother's breasts.

I was cast upon thee from the womb: thou art my God from my mother's belly.

(Psalm 22:9–10)

The LORD is my light and my salvation; whom shall I fear? the LORD is the strength of my life; of whom shall I be afraid?

One thing have I desired of the LORD, that will I seek after; that I may dwell in the house of the LORD all the days of my life, to behold the beauty of the LORD, and to inquire in his temple.

For in the time of trouble he shall hide me in his pavilion: in the secret of his tabernacle shall he hide me; he shall set me up upon a rock.

When my father and my mother forsake me, then the LORD will take me up.

(Psalm 27:1, 4–5, 10)

Thou art fairer than the children of men: grace is poured into thy lips: therefore God hath blessed thee for ever.

All thy garments smell of myrrh, and aloes, and cassia, out of the ivory palaces, whereby they have made thee glad. Kings' daughters were among thy honourable women: upon thy right hand did stand the queen in gold of Ophir.

Hearken, O daughter, and consider, and incline thine ear, forget also thine own people, and thy father's house; so shall the King greatly desire thy beauty. . . .

The king's daughter is all glorious within: her clothing is of wrought gold.

(Psalm 45:2, 8–9, 10–11, 13)

God is in the midst of her; she shall not be moved: God shall help her, and that right early.

(Psalm 46:5)

And I said, Oh that I had wings like a dove! for then would I fly away, and be at rest. Lo, then would I wander far off, and remain in the wilderness. Selah

For it was not an enemy that reproached me; then I could have borne it: neither was it he that hated me that did magnify himself against me; then I would have hid myself from him:

But it was thou, a man mine equal, my guide, and mine acquaintance.

We took sweet counsel together, and walked unto the house of God in company.

The words of his mouth were smoother than butter, but war was in his heart: his words were softer than oil, yet were they drawn swords.

(Psalm 55:6–7, 12–14, 21)

Be merciful unto me, O God: for man would swallow me up; he fighting daily oppresseth me.

(Psalm 56:1)

A father of the fatherless, and a judge of the widows, is God in his holy habitation.

God setteth the solitary in families: he bringeth out those which are bound with chains: but the rebellious dwell in a dry land.

(Psalm 68:5–6)

Cast me not off in the time of old age; forsake me not when my strength faileth.

Now also when I am old and greyheaded, O God, forsake me not; until I have shewed thy strength unto this generation, and thy power to every one that is to come.

(Psalm 71:9, 18)

LORD, thou hast been our dwelling place in all generations.

Before the mountains were brought forth, or ever thou hadst formed the earth and the world, even from everlasting to everlasting, thou art God.

And let the beauty of the LORD our God be upon us: and establish thou the work of our hands upon us; yea, the work of our hands establish thou it.

(Psalm 90:1–2, 17)

Yet setteth he the poor on high from affliction, and maketh him families like a flock.

(Psalm 107:41)

The LORD is on my side; I will not fear: what can man do unto me?

It is better to trust in the LORD than to put confidence in man.

It is better to trust in the LORD than to put confidence in princes.

(Psalm 118:6)

Whither shall I go from thy spirit? or whither shall I flee from thy presence?

If I ascend up into heaven, thou art there: if I make my bed in hell, behold, thou art there.

If I take the wings of the morning, and dwell in the uttermost parts of the sea;

Even there shall thy hand lead me, and thy right hand shall hold me.

(Psalm 139:7–10)

He healeth the broken in heart, and bindeth up their wounds.

(Psalm 147:3)

Chapter Eleven

The Widow, the Man and Jezebel

WHAT IF THE BIBLICAL GOD sends you the right man at the right time? Would you take him in?

Elijah is a case study of the appearance in your life of the right man at the right time. No journey through biblical consciousness is complete without visiting with Elijah. Moses and Jesus talk with Elijah on a *high mountain* (Matthew 17:1–13, Luke 9:28–36, Mark 9:2–13).

Both as an individual and as representative of key themes, Elijah is the archetypical male prophet of the Hebrew Bible. And no one likes him. Elijah is a prototype for Jesus' well-known statement delivered while preaching in his own hometown synagogue, *"No prophet is accepted in his hometown"* (Luke 4:24 *NIV*).

Elijah's prophetic ministry is described in part in 1 Kings. Times are terrible for the prophets. Where to go? To a woman, of course.

> *Then the word of the LORD came to him: "Go at once to Zarephath of Sidon and stay there. I have commanded a widow in that place to supply you with food." So he went to Zarephath. When he came to the town gate, a widow was there gathering sticks. He called to her and asked, "Would you bring me a little water in a jar so I may have a drink?"* (1 Kings 17:8–10 *NIV*)

She could have told him to get it himself. But verse 11 says, *As she was going to get it, he called, "And bring me, please, a piece of bread."*

Some might think this adds insult to injury. Others that biblical women are there only to serve men. But as we will see as we visit this story, the reverse is true. Elijah will serve her well, and God provides for both the male and female.

At the request of *bread* the woman tells Elijah that she has no *bread*. In fact all she has is a handful of flour in a barrel and a little oil in a container. What she is doing is gathering sticks for the last scrap of a meal for her son and herself. If, as the text has said, God has commanded this widow to sustain Elijah, she hasn't heard about it. She is at the end of her rope and ready to die. She can't see beyond the amount of food she has in the house.

What is the first thing Elijah says to her?

> *Fear not. . . .* (1 Kings 17:13)

Here again is the injunction to woman to *Fear not.* The first rule for solving whatever complexity, denial, or need you face is *Fear not.*

The second is to be hospitable. Elijah reminds her to entertain the stranger. He tells her to go home, make a small *bread* for him and then some for her and her son.

> *"For this is what the LORD, the God of Israel, says: 'The jar of flour will not be used up and the jug of oil will not run dry until the day the LORD gives rain on the land.' "*(1 Kings 17:14 *NIV*)

The oil is a symbol of anointing and prophecy and appears throughout the Bible; a look into your concordance will point you to those references. But there is more in this meeting of the powerless, starving woman and the unhappy, homeless male prophet. More even than the jug of oil that never fails.

> *Some time later the son of the woman who owned the house became ill. He grew worse and worse, and finally stopped breathing.* (1 Kings 17:17 *NIV*)

The woman thinks that her son's death is related to Elijah's visit. *"Did you come to remind me of my sin and kill my son?"* she asks. (1 Kings 17:18 *NIV*)

> *And he said unto her, Give me thy son. And he took him out of her bosom, and carried him up into a loft, where he abode, and laid him upon his own bed.*
>
> *And he stretched himself upon the child three times, and cried unto the LORD, and said, O LORD my God, I pray thee, let this child's soul come into him again.*
>
> *And the LORD heard the voice of Elijah; and the soul of the child came into him again, and he revived.*

And Elijah took the child, and brought him down out of the chamber into the house, and delivered him unto his mother: and Elijah said, See, thy son liveth. (1 Kings 17:19, 21–23)

The deep signification of this raising from the dead of a fatherless child needs to be contemplated quietly.

And the woman said to Elijah, Now by this I know that thou art a man of God, and that the word of the LORD in thy mouth is truth. (1 Kings 17:24)

It takes a woman, a widow, to recognize Elijah's truth. He is sustained by a seemingly powerless woman in his mission. You will see that women are often first to see what is visible only to inspired thought, often first to see Truth. And here is another woman in the long, long chain of biblical women, who recognize, affirm and set the seal on the activities of the word of the Lord.

But it is also a woman, Jezebel (making her first appearance in 1 Kings 16:31), who is the strongest enemy of Elijah. Jezebel has most of the Lord's prophets killed. Elijah challenges Jezebel's God, Baal. It is a contest over who and what is All. Baal worship claims to control fertility and *water.* Yet the prophets of Baal, who came with Jezebel from her native country to Israel when she married the king, cannot make it rain, no matter what. But *water* is Spirit's Word — an essential element of spiritual Creation. Elijah calls on the God of Israel, and then he slays Jezebel's false prophets with the sword. The rain comes (1 Kings 18:20–46).

From her ivory-towered palace, Queen Jezebel calls out for the death of Elijah within twenty-four hours. He goes where the prophets and children of Israel go, to the wilderness — to Horeb, where Moses and God spoke and where Moses received the Commandments. There Elijah hears God, *not in the wind, ... not in the earthquake, ... not in the fire, ...* but in *a still small voice,* a gentle whisper (1 Kings 19:11–12).

Jezebel, sensuousness incarnate, demands for her husband that which is not theirs — a neighbor's land. Writing letters in her husband's name, coveting her neighbor's property, breaking commandments, she has the owner and the heirs to the property stoned to death.

The Lord tells Elijah that Jezebel will be eaten by dogs (1 Kings 21:23). And she is. But not before her husband dies from wounds in battle, her two sons are murdered and, still unrepentant, she *painted her face,* fixed her hair and looked out a window to await and torment the army leader come to kill her. Jezebel's own eunuchs push her out the window in 2 Kings 9:30–33.

In the Bible, as in life, there are some greedy, power hungry, sensual women, as there are men. But Jezebel has not been condemned for her sexuality but for ignoring the mandate of hospitality. She has violated the law of kindness to strangers and made the fatal mistake of attacking a messenger of God. We will run into her name again in the Book of Revelation.

Here, there and everywhere

As one might expect from the Bible, the Lord's prophet Elijah is sustained in the wilderness by an angel of the Lord. Appearances on earth and in the cloud and who knows where are the meat of Elijah. His many encounters with women are central to his activity. When you read about him, you will see that he is here, there and everywhere, ready to find you or your nation in the most desperate moments.

Elijah takes consciousness to another dimension. He doesn't die; he arises to heaven on a chariot of fire. Elijah is outside chronological time. Look again to the *pillar of fire* that leads the Israelites for more on this.

If you look in the Bible to the book Mark, you will see Elijah (*Elias* in the New Testament) in another biblical example of simultaneous time:

> *And after six days Jesus taketh with him Peter, and James, and John, and leadeth them up into an high mountain apart by themselves: and he was transfigured before them. And his raiment became shining, exceeding white as snow; so as no fuller on earth can white them. And there appeared unto them Elias with Moses: and they were talking with Jesus.* (Mark 9:2–4)

The final biblical note on Elijah is in James 5:17: *Elias was a man subject to like passions as we are.*

So too are Amos, Daniel, Ezekiel, Ezra, Habakkuk, Haggai, Hosea, Isaiah, Jeremiah, Job, Joel, Jonah, Joshua, Malachi, Micah, Nahum, Nehemiah, Obadiah, Samuel, Zechariah and Zephaniah. The books of the Hebrew Bible named for these men show them to be of different temperaments, different styles. These men rant and rave and dream and see visions.

Trust your dreams, these men tell us. Your dreams are telling you about your life. These men share their dreams and visions with us and we learn much from their observations and prophecies about women and nations, about human nature and about a changing and growing perception of God in human consciousness.

Any summary fails the depths in the writings that bear their names. But it can be said that these prophets are often imperfect men. For example, Isaiah wanders naked in the wilderness, *goes into a prophetess* who conceives and bears a child. Jonah — to no avail — tries to run away from God. Most of these men go around telling everyone in graphic terms how horrible things are when *ruach Elohiym* is forgotten.

They also tell the people, and us, that God is the only Parent, gives conception, gives you what you ask for, provides female companionship, is gender free, is more patient and faithful than anyone on earth, loved you before you were in your mother's womb, heals all disease, keeps promises, feeds you in the wilderness for as long as you need, beards lions in their den, makes *water,* distributes it equally, provides *dry land,* is Love, Spirit, Truth, Mind, Life, Soul, All.

Isaiah calls Israel a harlot. Jeremiah, Ezekiel, Hosea, Joel, Amos, Micah and Nahum do the same thing. If you look up the words *harlot, harlotry,* you will find these references and not be at all surprised that there is little or no evidence that these men were popular. They said what no one wanted to hear.

If one views the prophets' association of whores with a city or a nation that turns away from the One God as attacks on womanhood, one misses the point. The point is not to condemn women. Rather, the point is brought home that God — and *male and female* — are inextricably associated with each other. And further, what a nation thinks about God has much to do with what a nation thinks about itself. And so the use of the word *harlot* is not just an attack on a nation's consciousness of itself but also on the idea that God is the province of any particular nation.

Further, as we look ahead to Revelation we will see that the figure of woman represents the struggle of all Israel — all those who strive. And we know we are headed in that direction and beyond — to an image of a pure, spiritual woman representing New Jerusalem. With that in mind we can recognize that, tiresome as these prophets may have seemed at the time, as ferocious as they often are to read, what they say is: Beware. Don't get sidetracked. Don't leave the spiritual union of *male and female* for idolatry.

Ezekiel specifically includes both men and women in his prophecies on individual responsibility and relationship to God. He also uses relationships between women as metaphors in prophecy. Of particular interest to women searching for their own relationship to God are Ezekiel 14:12–23 and chapter 16. Chapter 16 uses the relationship between lovers, husbands and wives, and sisters to discuss the difference between Eve's descendants and the *female* of *male and female* in Genesis 1:27.

Chapter 17 of Ezekiel is put forth as a parable. You see in the chapter words and images already familiar from your trip so far through the Bible: *wings, seed, vine, tree* are some. Though Ezekiel is often read as a treatise on the politics and devotion of nations or a prefiguration of Revelation, it can easily be read as an address to your own thought. Its language is the language of women's relationships, hopes and fears.

If you are reading a Bible that contains divisions of Old and New Testament, you will see that in the last twelve books of the Old Testament all the images and themes and promises of the Bible are recapped and prophesied.

Micah says:

In that day, saith the LORD, will I assemble her that halteth, and I will gather her that is driven out, and her that I have afflicted;

And I will make her that halted a remnant, and her that was cast far off a strong nation. . . .

And thou, O tower of the flock, the strong hold of the daughter of Zion, unto thee shall it come, even the first dominion; the kingdom shall come to the daughter of Jerusalem.

Now why dost thou cry out aloud? is there no king in thee? is thy counsellor perished? for pangs have taken thee as a woman in travail. (Micah 4:6–9)

Jonah is a story not to be missed. It's not just a story of a man living in the belly of a whale. Jonah is commentary on spiritual Creation. And too, the story of Jonah addresses the reluctance and resistance of those who must fulfill their mission.

But before Jonah fulfills his mission, Esther will fulfill hers.

Chapter Twelve

The Queens

ARE YOU AFRAID TO STAND UP FOR YOURSELF? Do you think personal happiness is your only reason for being born?

Let's look at Esther and the second of the two books in the Bible named for women. Like Ruth, Esther lives among foreigners. Ruth saves the day for the biological line of the children of Israel, and Esther saves the day for the people of Israel as a whole.

But where Ruth is a Moabitess, Esther is, by birth, a Jew and a woman with her own holiday. Her story is celebrated each year as Purim.

The Book of Esther describes how men in power fear women and Jews. It's got love, danger and an upsetting of the best-laid plans of an evil, boastful, self-serving man. Esther is a great story for a rainy afternoon, and it does no disservice to its religious importance to read it as a wonderful short story. There is an orphan heroine who lives in a palace. And what a palace! The descriptions of the white, green and blue hangings, the pillars of marble, the beds of gold and silver, the floors of red, blue, white and black marble, the gold wineglasses will take you, for a time, out of the everyday.

The device that sets up Esther's story is the demand of a husband, a king, whose *heart was made merry by wine* (Esther 1:10) and the refusal of a wife, a queen, to be put on public display solely for her physical beauty.

You'll see as you read that we are not told whether female beauty is reflected in black skin or white or brown or a mixture or whether beauty is measured in height as 5'6" or 6'2" or 4'10", or weight of one hundred, two hundred or three hundred pounds. Rather, this story, and the Bible as a whole, seldom describes how women or men look but instead how they think, what they wonder, how they respond and what they do.

119

Ahasuerus, the king who reigned from India to Ethiopia, commanded

> *to bring Vashti the queen before the king with the crown royal,*
> *to shew the people and the princes her beauty; for she was fair to*
> *look on. But the queen Vashti refused to come at the king's com-*
> *mandment by his chamberlains: therefore was the king very*
> *wroth, and his anger burned in him.* (Esther 1:11–12)

Call her independent, call her a liberated woman, Vashti's refusal to come when she was called evokes the rage some men have when they can't control women. The king traps himself when he makes public a call for his wife to appear at his bidding. He is humiliated in public. As we know today, some men fear this, and think that lack of obedience is known to others and undermines their power.

So, rather than deal with his wife on a one-to-one basis, the king, full of himself and his power, asks his wise men what to do. Although the Bible text expresses no judgment at all on Vashti's refusal, the men in power all agree that she has committed an offense that, if other women hear of it, will cause women to despise their husbands and *there arise too much contempt and wrath* (Esther 1:18). The men advise the king to change queens quickly and give Vashti's royal estate to another woman. And they make a law that every man shall bear rule in his own house (Esther 1:22).

What are women to make of this story? Certainly that the men want absolute control over women. Certainly that men fear a woman seen as making her own decisions. Certainly that men use money as a weapon, and that men feel legislation is the sure way to deal with their fears.

> *After these things, when the anger of King Ahasuerus had*
> *abated, he remembered Vashti, and what she had done and*
> *what had been decreed against her.* (Esther 2:1 *NRSV*)

The king feels better because he has exercised authority. But look at the word *remembered.* You know the biblical use of this word most often brings spiritual fulfillment. Does this mean that the king gave Vashti her own household? Does it mean he treated her well? Did she take her royal belongings and move? Did she stay there? The reader might look to see if the Bible says Vashti lost anything but that which she did not want — an appearance before the king, who had been drinking. The fact is, without Vashti's independence there would be no room in the palace for the woman to come. Women pave the way for other women and, as far as the biblical text goes, lose nothing in doing so.

The search begins for a virgin to take the queen's place. Enter Esther. Her rise to power and what she did with it is a story that holds great and timeless appeal to some. Others simply can't stand Esther. The Book of Esther evokes, among other things, a strong response as to how women should act. And Vashti's refusal to come when called is mild compared to what Esther does when she has power. There is reason for vain men in power to fear women.

A monumentally significant point is made in chapter 4, verse 14; if you read only one line of this book of the Bible, you should read the question: *Who knows whether you are come to the kingdom for such a time as this?*

Whenever you have doubts about your role in life, your plans, your work, your nation, your temple or church, ask yourself this question. Read it in the context of the story and think about your connections to the rest of the human family. Reason on your potential.

You'll see in the story of Esther that fear of women who refuse to obey the men in power shifts to fear of Jews. Mordecai, a Jew and Esther's nearest living relative, refuses to come before the king, refuses to bow down to Hamman, a powerful favorite of the king. He echoes Vashti's action. And so Hamman orders all the Jews killed. As a woman and a Jew, Esther is the potential focus of the hatred and fear. But Esther is in a line of biblical women who demonstrate that hatred of women or Jews is not acceptable to God.

Although Esther makes no reference to God by name, there are references to the elements and characteristics of God everywhere in the story.

After you've read the ten chapters of the story through for its drama, read the story again with your notebook. Mark down the words you know that tell you that you are not only in a Middle Eastern palace-cum-harem but in spiritual territory.

Seven days, remembered, abundance, seed, grace, favour, light, joy are just a few such words. *Virgin, sackcloth, ashes, rending of clothes, myrrh* are others in Esther's story that appear in key events throughout the Bible.

As both Vashti and Mordecai refuse to bow to secular power,

some experienced Bible readers see the story as one stressing obedience to God, not the state. Others take the king to be a metaphor
for God or view the king and Esther as representing the union of
the masculine and feminine elements necessary for harmony and
peace. Others still think Esther is a tool of men and their sexuality
but concede that, at the very least, she is at the right place at the right
time. She saves lives.

Esther's story is dramatic. She emerges as a major player in the
unfolding of biblical drama and as a woman who lives today in
countless hearts and minds as a role model. But, as in all the Bible
says about women, there is so much more to her story than a surface
reading indicates. There are spiritual depths to be plumbed in the
tale of Esther, and you and your daughters and sons have at hand the
joy of discovering what she tells you about woman's triumph over
hatred. She also tells us that each woman has a specific purpose
in life.

Ask yourself, "What is my purpose?"

Chapter Thirteen

The Struggle Within

WHAT IF THE STORY OF JOB is not a struggle between God and the devil over a man's soul? What if the story represents your own wrestling with Spirit today? What if the story means that the God/Spirit of all Creation is speaking to you — now — in a voice that is as female as male?

The story of the man who is remembered more for his boils than for almost anything else is an exploration into the struggle of consciousness to understand and acknowledge God. Not to be over-looked in the story is that women are once more elevated to their natural rights.

Where once the tale of Job was used to justify a vexing God who tests men and women or visits bad things on good people, Job's experience is now most often viewed as taking place in his own thought. As he puts it, *The thing which I greatly feared has come upon me* (Job 3:25).

> For Job thought, "Perhaps my children have sinned and blasphemed God in their thoughts." This is what Job always used to do. (Job 1:5 *TNK*)

Job is afraid for his children, and when he receives reports — and they are only reports — from messengers that he has lost everything, he tears his clothes, shaves his head, falls on the ground and worships (Job 1:20).

Once the situation is set up, it takes over thirty chapters for Job to lament, question and examine what he believes has happened to him and what, if anything, he can do about it. This is meant to be a public discourse. Job wants everyone to know his agony:

> How I wish that someone would remember my words and record them in a book! (Job 19:23 *GNB*)

123

Job has three friends, and in an older perspective on the story, the *three friends* represent three different approaches to understanding God. In the present view, the *friends* are different aspects of Job's own thought about God.

As you read, you will rediscover for yourself many popular theologies in Job's questioning — and in his *friends'* comments. Theologians and churches have spent much time dissecting the arguments and positions taken by the men. But our interest is in what God has to say. Let's pick up Job's struggle in chapter 38 — at the point where the Divine speaks out on spiritual Creation.

Listen to the authority of the voice of the Spirit that moved on the face of the *waters* speaking to Job. Do you assume the voice to be male? When you read these words of God from your Bible, hear how they sound in a woman's voice:

"Who is this that darkens my counsel with words without knowledge? Brace yourself like a man; I will question you, and you shall answer me." (Job 38:2 *NIV*)

Put yourself in Job's place. Picture yourself being asked these questions by the female aspect of Spirit.

If you are a man, try to hear the words as if your mother were asking you the questions.

If you are a woman, read the following out loud from your own Bible to hear what the female voice sounds like as Spirit asks the ageless, profound questions:

> *Where were you when I laid the earth's foundation?*
> *Tell me, if you understand.*
> *Who marked off its dimensions? Surely you know!*
> *Who stretched a measuring line across it?*
> *On what were its footings set, or who laid its cornerstone—*
> *while the morning stars sang together and all the angels shouted for joy?*
> *Who shut up the sea behind doors when it burst forth from the womb . . . ?*
> *Have you ever given orders to the morning, or shown the dawn its place . . . ?*
> *Have you journeyed the springs of the sea or walked in the recesses of the deep?*

What is the way to the abode of light?
Surely you know, for you were already born!
                                   (Job 38:4–7, 8, 12, 16, 19, 21 *NIV*)

Think back to spiritual Creation and *water* as you ask yourself
this question and hear directly the inquiry from Spirit:

Hast thou entered into the treasures of the snow? or hast thou
seen the treasures of the hail, which I have reserved against
the time of trouble, against the day of battle and war? (Job
38:22–23)

Go back to *light.*

By what way is the light parted, which scattereth the east wind
upon the earth?
   Hath the rain a father? Or who hath begotten the drops of
dew?
   Out of whose womb came the ice? And the hoary frost of
heaven, who hath gendered it? (Job 38:24, 28–29)

Think of the fourth day of Creation.

Canst thou bind the sweet influences of Pleiades, or loose the
bands of Orion?
   Canst thou bring forth Mazzaroth in his season? Or canst
thou guide Arcturus with his sons? (Job 38:31–32)

Look to the sixth day.

Knowest thou the ordinances of heaven? Canst thou set the
dominion thereof in the earth? (Job 38:33)

Back to the *waters, abundance,* the *flood,* Moses.

Canst thou lift up thy voice to the clouds, that abundance of
waters may cover thee?
   Canst thou send lightnings, that they may go, and say unto
thee, Here we are? (Job 38:34–35)

Think again of Lebanon.

Who hath put wisdom in the inward parts? Or who hath given
understanding to the heart? (Job 38:36)

How will you answer these questions?
God gives the answer:

Deck now thyself with majesty and excellency; and array thyself with glory and beauty. (Job 40:10)

If you wrap yourself in the *glory*, it is possible to see the strength and *dominion* God gave you before you were even born. All one has comes from the Maker.

Then will I also confess unto thee that thine own right hand can save thee. (Job 40 :14)

If you didn't look into the symbolic use of *right hand* when you read about Rachel's son, Benjamin, you'll want to see here what the Bible has to say about that *right hand*.

I know that thou canst do every thing, and that no thought can be withholden from thee, Job 42:2 says.

Wrestling with your own understanding of God you may, like Job, see and understand *things too wonderful for me* (Job 42:3).

This *wonderful* understanding of God beyond guilt, blame, equivocation and suffering results in the blessing of Creation:

So the LORD blessed the latter end of Job more than his beginning: for he had fourteen thousand sheep, and six thousand camels, and a thousand yoke of oxen, and a thousand she asses. He had also seven sons and three daughters. And he called the name of the first, Jemima; and the name of the second, Kezia; and the name of the third, Kerenhappuch. And in all the land were no women found so fair as the daughters of Job: and their father gave them inheritance among their brethren. (Job 42:12–15)

Job's fear is gone. His children are alive, and his daughters and sons both receive inheritance. In the consciousness of the Creator, of Spirit, *male and female* are equal, and as in Job's account — as in the first chapter of Genesis — female is the final idea mentioned.

Chapter Fourteen

Crying in the Wilderness

WHO IS YOUR HUSBAND? Isaiah answers that question.

The Book of Isaiah speaks to all people in all times: *learn to do well; seek judgment, relieve the oppressed, judge the fatherless, plead for the widow* (Isaiah 1:17).

There are references in Isaiah to everything from spiritual Creation to Adam and Eve and to the Book of Revelation. There are references to Abraham and Sarah, to Egypt, the Commandments, the *cloud,* the *tabernacle,* Israel, *the woman in travail, cities,* the practice of religion and the fulfillment of prophecy. There are references to *the new heaven and the new earth,* and to *wiping away all tears from the eyes.* There are parables, visions, oracles and promises. Isaiah is a poem that speaks to every heart in every age.

A passage you may want to take a look at opens chapter 4 of Isaiah:

And in that day seven women shall take hold of one man, saying, We will eat our own bread, and wear our own apparel: only let us be called by thy name, to take away our reproach.

(Isaiah 4:1)

Whether the seven women represent the sign of completeness, or the Sabbath day of rest of Creation, or whether they are the seven women prophets of Israel or any other seven women is up to the reader. The reader who puts together the seven women with the one man will come up with eight — the number of people that went into safety from the flood in the ark — a number representing complete disappearance of any discord or fear, a place beyond even the seven representing completeness.

No matter how many fine points are put to it, the inescapable point is also that in the day when women are recognized as equal, when women eat their own bread, wear their own clothes, are called by the name that belongs to them; on the day of full acceptance of spirituality, when women are given their full rights and their spiritual names, that will be the day when safety is a given and God dwells unmistakably among us. And not until then.

Back to the waters

Isaiah has lots of comfort but also lots of upbraiding the people in vigorous terms to forget Adam and turn to the God of spiritual Creation.

> *Cease ye from man, who breath is in his nostrils, for wherein is he to be accounted of?* (Isaiah 2:22)

So much for Adam.
Look at the comfort:

> *Since thou wast precious in my sight, thou hast been honorable, and I have loved thee: therefore will I give men for thee, and people for thy life.* (Isaiah 43:4)

And look at the nature of God and the people's relationship:

> *Hast thou not known? hast thou not heard, that the everlasting God, the LORD, the Creator of the ends of the earth, fainteth not, neither is weary? there is no searching of his understanding. He giveth power to the faint; and to them that have no might he increaseth strength. Even the youths shall faint and be weary, and the young men shall utterly fall: but they that wait upon the LORD shall renew their strength; they shall mount up with wings as eagles; they shall run, and not be weary; and they shall walk, and not faint.* (Isaiah 40:28–31)

Images from Isaiah emerge again in Revelation 12:14. You will see there the eagle, and in Revelation 22:17 an invitation recalling this one:

> *Ho, every one that thirsteth, come ye to the waters, and he that hath no money; come ye, buy, and eat; yea, come, buy wine and milk without money and without price.* (Isaiah 55:1)

God — through Isaiah — assures us: *As one whom his mother comforteth, so will I comfort you; and ye shall be comforted in Jerusalem* (Isaiah 66:13).

There are further assurances of comfort and companionship and a clear sense of the all-presence of God:

Fear not: for I am with thee: I will bring thy seed from the east, and gather thee from the west; I will say to the north, Give up; and to the south, Keep not back: bring my sons from far, and my daughters from the ends of the earth. (Isaiah 43:5–6)

Inspired by Isaiah, Handel wrote his oratorio *The Messiah*.

Comfort ye, comfort ye my people, saith your God. (Isaiah 40:1)

O Zion, that bringest good tidings, get thee up into the high mountain; O Jerusalem, that bringest good tidings, lift up thy voice with strength; lift it up, be not afraid; say unto the cities of Judah, Behold your God! (Isaiah 40:9)

You will want to read chapter 54 for yourself. It is a song to womanhood, an incomparable comfort. Perhaps you can craft an oratorio from its verses.

For thy Maker is thine husband. . . . (Isaiah 54:5)

And all thy children shall be taught of the LORD; and great shall be the peace of thy children. (Isaiah 54:13)

No weapon that is formed against thee shall prosper; and every tongue that shall rise against thee in judgment thou shalt condemn. This is the heritage of the servants of the LORD, and their righteousness is of me, saith the LORD. (Isaiah 54:17)

The last chapter of Isaiah repeats the theme of the woman in travail:

Before she travailed, she brought forth; before her pain came, she was delivered of a man child.

Who hath heard such a thing? who hath seen such things? Shall the earth be made to bring forth in one day? or shall a nation be born at once? for as soon as Zion travailed, she brought forth her children.

Shall I bring to the birth, and not cause to bring forth? saith the LORD: shall I cause to bring forth, and shut the womb? saith thy God. (Isaiah 66:7–9)

Listen here as God as Mother speaks:

Rejoice ye with Jerusalem, and be glad with her, all ye that love her: rejoice for joy with her, all ye that mourn for her:

That ye may suck, and be satisfied with the breasts of her consolations; that ye may milk out, and be delighted with the abundance of her glory.

For thus saith the LORD, Behold, I will extend peace to her like a river, and the glory of the Gentiles like a flowing stream: then shall ye suck, ye shall be borne upon her sides, and be dandled upon her knees. For I know their works and their thoughts: it shall come, that I will gather all nations and tongues; and they shall come, and see my glory. (Isaiah 66:10–12, 18)

Isaiah is read as prophecy of the Messiah. As you read the Book of Isaiah, you might want to underline the places that speak to you of the Messiah. Finding those verses and those threads for yourself is preparation for life in the holy city.

Chapter Fifteen

Deep Waters

THERE ARE THOSE DAYS when moods can overtake you. There are those days in a life when nothing works, when unrequited love, sadness, depression and despair seem to be the entire landscape of thought. What you want is not there and what you usually do to lift yourself out of it — a hot bath, a long talk with a friend, a movie, shopping, work, a run around the block — isn't available or doesn't work.

You feel as if Adam and Eve really did bring punishment through the ages — right down to your doorstep. You seem stuck in strange genetic coding traits inherited from your family through the generations, convinced almost that genes are programmed to use human beings to secure the continuity of genes themselves. And this leaves you helpless and hopeless.

Curl up in bed with the Song of Songs. (If your Bible doesn't have this book, go find a Bible that does.)

The eight chapters that make up this book are full of joy, intimacy, physical description, passion and sensuousness. Whether one reads it straight as it is written or takes it to be an allegory of God's love for Israel, the Song of Songs (or the Song of Solomon as the King James Version calls it) is sexually explicit. And the body is celebrated.

All in all this is a book for the imaginative woman. It resounds with love. Curling up in bed with the Song of Songs, lingering over the detailed descriptions you find there, provides eroticism with inspiration. The text is just as juicy as a popular novel and much more descriptive in its imagery.

There is no shame in the Song of Songs. No sin, no guilt. No Eve.

Kisses, delights, sweet smells, anticipation, eagerness — the text spills over with desire for love and the beloved.

This centerpiece of the Hebrew Bible is required reading for anyone who thinks the Book is a proscriptive sexist text. Imagine, if you choose, God as your lover, or you and your lover as worshiping God together, or read it any way you want. Excerpts don't do it justice. Read it for yourself. No one is looking over your shoulder. The text speaks directly to you.

A completely other approach

If the Song of Songs isn't an antidote to whatever ails you, throw yourself into the Book of Lamentations. It speaks directly to women who are burdened. It recognizes the way you feel, and that recognition takes away the sting of being misunderstood and abandoned.

Just the first six verses of Lamentations address the state of widowhood, weeping, loss of lovers, friends who betray, life among the heathen, children in captivity to enemies, faded beauty and lack of leadership. Lamentations says that there are things in life to weep over and that when those days come:

> *Cry unto the LORD*
> *wail, O daughter of Zion;*
> *Weep tears like a torrent,*
> *day and night;*
> *Give yourself no respite;*
> *let your tears cease not.*
> (Lamentations 2:18 *AT*)

Read yearly in temple during midsummer on the ninth of Av (Tishah B'Av), Lamentations commemorates, in a mournful celebration, the destruction of the First and Second Temples. But a broader and more immediate significance to Lamentations can be found when you look at the themes of destruction and loss in a very personal way. Read it as it is written with all the "shes" and "hers" and female imagery as empathizing with you.

The first verses set the tone.

> *How lonely sits the city that once was full of people! How like a widow she has become, she that was great among the nations! She that was a princess among the provinces has become a vassal.*
> *She weeps bitterly in the night, with tears on her cheeks; among all her lovers she has no one to comfort her; all her*

friends have dealt treacherously with her, they have become her enemies. (Lamentations 1–2 *NRSV*)

Have you ever felt this way?
Or this way?

For these things I weep; my eyes flow with tears; for a comforter is far from me, one to revive my courage; my children are desolate, for the enemy has prevailed.
                                                      (Lamentations 1:16 *NRSV*)

Or:

I have forgotten what happiness is . . .
                                                      (Lamentations 3:17 *NRSV*)

But after a little wallowing, things look up by chapter 3. Look at these verses:

This I recall to my mind, therefore have I hope. It is of the LORD's mercies that we are not consumed, because his compassions fail not. They are new every morning: great is thy faithfulness. The LORD is my portion, sayeth my soul; therefore will I hope in him. The LORD is good unto them that wait for him, to the soul that seeketh him. (Lamentations 3:21–25)

The ebbing and flowing of moods, thoughts and experience is plain in Lamentations. Things were once great, then they are terrible, then they get better and then worse again. But by the end of the book there is a balance of thought, an acceptance. In your darkest hours read Lamentations and see if the same thing doesn't happen for you.

Read not as history, nor as condemnation of women, rather as a voice through the ages that understands your mourning, your need, Lamentations can at least, in its sense of suffering and loss, bring you face to face with the honest recognition that if things can't get any worse, then they have to get better.

Interesting times

Lamentations is properly called the Lamentations of Jeremiah. Like Huldah, Jeremiah lived during the reign of King Josiah, and it is interesting to note that then a female interpreted the Law and a male prophesied in female imagery.

Jeremiah is often depicted as a frightening figure. But his first report of the word of the Lord is: *Before I formed thee in the belly I knew thee; and before thou camest forth out of the womb I sanctified thee, and I ordained thee a prophet unto the nations* (Jeremiah 1:5).

Sure of spiritual conception and his individualized identity outside of chronological time, Jeremiah speaks to all when he speaks of gathering *families* (Jeremiah 1:15), compares the *daughter of Zion to a comely and delicate woman* (Jeremiah 6:2), and says bluntly: *They have healed also the hurt of the daughter of my people slightly, saying, Peace, peace; when there is no peace* (Jeremiah 6:14, 8:11).

Jeremiah suffers like a mother and complains to God:

> *Many pastors have destroyed my vineyard, they have trodden my portion underfoot, they have made my pleasant portion a desolate wilderness. They have made it desolate, and being desolate it mourneth unto me; the whole land is made desolate, because no man layeth it to heart.* (Jeremiah 12:10–11)

Jeremiah is told to write: *Thus speaketh the LORD God of Israel, saying, Write thee all the words that I have spoken unto thee in a book.* (Jeremiah 30:2)

What follows in chapters 30 and 31 contains some of the Bible's most poignant pages. The promises of the Lord are wrought in images that speak deeply to your relationships, your heart and your hopes. You will want to spend time pondering what Jeremiah has written.

Here is a small sample from these two chapters.

> *Ask ye now, and see whether a man doth travail with child? wherefore do I see every man with his hands on his loins, as a woman in travail, and all faces are turned into paleness?*
> (Jeremiah 30:6)

> *For I am with thee, saith the LORD, to save thee: though I make a full end of all nations whither I have scattered thee, yet will I not make a full end of thee: but I will correct thee in measure, and will not leave thee altogether unpunished.* (Jeremiah 30:11)

> *For I will restore health unto thee and I will heal thee of thy wounds, saith the LORD; because they called thee an Outcast, saying, This is Zion, whom no man seeketh after.*
> (Jeremiah 30:17)

The LORD hath appeared of old unto me saying, Yea, I have loved thee with an everlasting love: therefore with lovingkindness have I drawn thee. (Jeremiah 31:3)

Behold, I will bring them from the north country, and gather them from the coasts of the earth, and with them the blind and the lame, the woman with child and her that travaileth with child together: a great company shall return thither.
                                                            (Jeremiah 31:8)

Set thee up waymarks, make thee high heaps: set thine heart toward the highway, even the way which thou wentest: turn again, O virgin of Israel, turn again to these thy cities.

How long wilt thou go about, O thou backsliding daughter? for the LORD hath created a new thing in the earth, A woman shall compass a man. (Jeremiah 31:21–22)

For I have satiated the weary soul, and I have replenished every sorrowful soul. (Jeremiah 31:25)

Chapter Sixteen

In the Temple

WHAT IF THE BIBLE SAYS a priest has to go to a woman to find out what the Word of God actually says?

That is precisely what happens in the story of Huldah.

Huldah is a prophetess, the chosen voice of the Lord.

King Josiah has been shown the book of the Law, which has been lost and then found during repairs to the house of the Lord (2 Kings 22:8). Josiah, still in his twenties when he is shown the recovered book, rends his clothes when he hears its words, realizing that *our fathers* haven't listened to or obeyed the words. Looking for the true interpretation of the Teaching, he sends men who represent different classes in society, saying, *Go,* to a priest, a scribe, a servant and two other men, . . . *and inquire of the LORD for me, and for the people, and for all Judah, concerning the words of this book that is found* (2 Kings 22:13).

Huldah is where they go to find the voice of the Lord, not only for the king but for the priests, the servants, the scribes and for all Judah. She is dwelling in *Jerusalem in the college* (2 Kings 22:14). She speaks for the Lord and looks to be, according to the biblical text, the only person on earth who can interpret God's Word.

Without a second thought she interprets the book:

And she said unto them, Thus saith the LORD God of Israel, Tell the man that sent you to me, Thus saith the LORD, Behold, I will bring evil upon this place, and upon the inhabitants thereof, even all the words of the book which the king of Judah hath read: Because they have forsaken me, and have burned incense unto other gods, that they might provoke me to anger with all the works of their hands; therefore my wrath shall be kindled against this place, and shall not be quenched. But to the king of Judah which sent you to inquire of the LORD, thus

136

shall ye say to him, Thus saith the LORD God of Israel, As touch-
ing the words which thou hast heard; Because thine heart was
tender, and thou hast humbled thyself before the LORD, when
thou heardest what I spake against this place, and against the
inhabitants thereof, that they should become a desolation and
a curse, and hast rent thy clothes, and wept before me; I also
have heard thee, saith the LORD. Behold therefore, I will gather
thee unto thy fathers, and thou shalt be gathered into thy grave
in peace; and thine eyes shall not see all the evil which I will
bring upon this place. And they brought the king word again.
(2 Kings 22:15–20)

Huldah's speaking for the Lord causes a turnaround in the thinking, observances and practices of the entire kingdom, restoring
Passover observance and causing the king to put magicians, wiz-
ards and idols out of the land. There was no king before or after
him, the Bible says, *that turned to the LORD with all his heart, and*
with all his soul, and with all his might, according to all the law of
Moses (2 Kings 23:23–25). Thanks to Huldah.

The Bible makes clear in this story that a woman is fully qualified
to understand, interpret and speak for the Lord, the Supreme Ruler.
There is more about this Huldah story, a repeated form (2 Chronicles
34) for those readers who might enjoy digging into this profoundly
important record of a woman who interprets the holy texts of Israel.

Along with Sarah, Miriam, Deborah, Hannah, Abigail and Esther,
Huldah is one of Israel's seven women prophets. Huldah's prophetic
place in Scripture, however, differs from that of the other women
prophets. Each woman has her place in prophecy, but Huldah is
the only one of them who unveils God's meaning directly from the
written text.

And the Hebrew Bible closes with Huldah and the implications
of her interpretation. Please note that while the Hebrew Bible closes
with 2 Chronicles, the Old Testament of the Christian Bible includes
additional writings of the Prophets, the last one being Malachi.

But there is more to come. We turn now to the New Testament,
which recounts the life and works of Jesus Christ, describes the history of the early church and depicts in the Book of Revelation the
struggles for consciousness.

Chapter Seventeen

Who Tells the Story?

WHAT DO YOU THINK ABOUT JESUS? Do you think that He is God? Or another of many great and learned men? Whatever you think or feel about Mary's son Jesus, the focus of the New Testament is Jesus: what he did and said, how people reacted to the man, what the implications are for women and men and for the individual who reflects on the meaning of Jesus' life in relation to her own life.

Whatever one thinks about the person of Jesus — whether one thinks he was a man; a prophet in a long line of prophets; God, who for a time made Himself into a man and came down to earth; the personification of the Christ — studying the character of the man and the events of the life described in the gospels is the way to know for yourself: Study can broaden both a historical and personal sense of the man who says:

- *My Father worketh hitherto, and I work.* (John 5:17)

- *I am the living bread which came down from heaven.* (John 6:51)

- *Before Abraham was, I Am.* (John 8:58)

- *I am the light of the world.* (John 9:5)

- *I am the good shepherd.* (John 10:11)

- *I and my Father are one.* (John 10:30)

- *I am the way, the truth, and the life.* (John 14:16)

- *I am the true vine, and my Father is the husbandman.* (John 15:1)

The life of Jesus the Christ or Christ Jesus (*Jesus,* as in Joshua, meaning "Savior"; *Christ* meaning "anointed one," or Messias) is told to us in many ways. Four different versions of Jesus' life, work and sayings address four different ways of thinking; these four versions are called the *gospels* — a word that means "good news." The authors tell us some (but not all) of the same stories about Jesus, but they are told from quite different perspectives.

The last gospel — the Gospel of John — begins with the spiritual Creation of the first chapter of Genesis: *In the beginning was the Word, and the Word was with God, and the Word was God* (John 1:1). John talks about *Light,* then he introduces John the Baptist and by chapter 2 (with no discussion of Jesus' birth or youth) has us at the opening of Jesus' ministry where the *water* is turned to *wine.*

The first gospel is the Gospel of Matthew. Matthew was a tax collector, and his account of Jesus begins with a genealogical list of the *generation of Jesus Christ* (Matthew 1:1) — Abraham to Jesus, forty-two in all. And then there is a brief account of the birth of Jesus from the point of view of Joseph. By placing Jesus in a line of male "begats," Matthew's version pretty much reflects the cultural mindset of any day. Matthew is the only one of the four gospel authors who recounts the trip to Egypt to save the baby Jesus from Herod (Matthew 2:13–16). It is Matthew who repeats Jeremiah's *Rachel weeping for her children* (Matthew 2:18).

Mark allegedly talked to Jesus' disciple Peter. Mark's version begins with John the Baptist clothed with camel's hair and with a girdle of skin about his loins, eating locusts and wild honey and preaching in the wilderness the baptism of repentance as he announces the appearance of one *who shall baptize you with the Holy Ghost* (Mark 1:2–8). Mark's account has Jesus make his entrance as a full-grown man (Mark 1:9). He gives no record of any part of Jesus' childhood or adolescence.

Luke says he interviewed the eyewitnesses (Luke 1:2). Many of the eyewitnesses were women, and Luke's account begins with Elisabeth and her conception of Jesus' cousin, John the Baptist. Mary's response to the angelic announcement that she will conceive is in Luke.

Did the angel appear to Joseph or to Mary?

Matthew says an unnamed angel appeared in a dream to Joseph. Luke says the angel Gabriel visited Mary at her home. Let's take a closer look at Luke's account. It's not as metaphysical and abstract as John's, not as worldly as Matthew's and not as perfunctory as Mark's.

Luke begins with the story of Elisabeth and her husband Zacharias (Luke 1:5–25). Elisabeth is a descendant of Miriam's and Moses' brother, Aaron. Elisabeth is barren and, like Sarah, of advanced age. An angel appears to her husband Zacharias and tells him that Elisabeth will bear a son who must be named John (Luke 1:13). And this is not to be just any son but one who is *great in the sight of the LORD* (Luke 1:15). Zacharias wants to know how he will know this is true (Luke 1:18).

The angel answers, *"I am Gabriel. I stand in the very presence of God. I have been sent to speak to you and to tell you this good news. Now you will keep silent and be unable to speak . . . "* (Luke 1:19–20 *AT*).

Elisabeth keeps herself shut up for five months, perhaps to avoid neighbors' gossip and speculation. In the sixth month — and you will remember that the sixth day is the day that male and female were created — the angel Gabriel goes from God to Mary and says, *Hail, thou that art highly favoured, the Lord is with thee; blessed art thou among women* (Luke 1:28).

Mary, like any woman might, wonders what this all means: *Mary was deeply perturbed at these words and wondered what such a greeting could possibly mean* (Luke 1:29 *Phillips*).

And the angel says to her what Elijah said to the widow, what the angel said to Hagar, what Gabriel said to Zacharias, what angels say to men and women through all time, *Fear not* (Luke 1:30).

Then comes the announcement that she will have a child, who will reign over the house of Jacob forever.

Still, she asks the question that is being asked to this day.

How shall this be, seeing I know not a man? (Luke 1:34). Gabriel explains how this will happen: *The holy Ghost shall come upon thee, and the power of the Highest shall overshadow thee* (Luke 1:35).

And then, for "proof in the flesh," Gabriel tells her about Elisabeth and adds the line that says it all: *For with God nothing shall be impossible* (Luke 1:37).

And echoing Ruth and Hannah and Abigail, Mary says, *Behold the handmaid of the Lord; be it unto me according to thy word* (Luke 1:38).

Phillips translates her response as *"I belong to the Lord, body and soul, let it happen as you say"* (Luke 1:38).

The next thing she does (Luke 1:39–40) makes such sense that it's hard to believe that Luke didn't get this story from Mary herself.

She gets up and goes to see Elisabeth, her cousin. Read for yourself the surface story of what Elisabeth and Mary talked about. Think about what it must have been like to be these women, speculating for three months on their pregnancies, their children, their future, the cost and the price of these two conceptions. See where Elisabeth says to Mary, *blessed is the fruit of thy womb* (Luke 1:42). Ponder the third day of creation where not only *fruit* springs forth but *the seed is within itself.* *"But God giveth it a body as it hath pleased him, and to every seed his own body,"* the Bible says later by way of further explanation (1 Corinthians 15:38).

See another step in the process of both redeeming and demythologizing Eve when Mary paraphrases Hannah's song in her response to Elisabeth (Luke 1:46–55). Here's another instance of women talking with and to women through the ages.

And, after abiding together three months, the women part. Mary returns to her *house* and the story cuts back to the birth and naming of Elisabeth's child:

> *When the eighth day came, they were going to circumcise the child and call him Zacharias, after his father, but his mother said, "Oh, no! he must be called John."*
> *"But none of your relations is called John," they replied.*
> (Luke 1:59–61 *Phillips*)

Although the bystanders in the temple where the scene takes place may not understand, the reader knows that the child is not the product solely of biological reproduction. His name — "to whom Jehovah is gracious" — is meant to reflect that spiritual conception.

> *And they made signs to his father to see what name he wanted the child to have. He beckoned for a writing-tablet and wrote the words, "His name is John," which greatly surprised everybody. Then his power of speech suddenly came back, and his first words were to thank God.* (Luke 1:62–64 *Phillips*)

And not long after, Mary *brought forth her firstborn son, and wrapped him in swaddling clothes, and laid him in a manger; because there was no room for them in the inn* (Luke 2:7).

The *shepherds abiding in the field,* the *angel of the Lord,* the *glory of the Lord* shining round about them, the *good tidings of great joy* and the *multitude of the heavenly host praising God and saying,*

> *Glory to God in the highest,*
> *and on earth peace,*
> *good will toward men*

— all the wonder is described by Luke (Luke 2:8–14).

But Mary kept all these things, and pondered them in her heart (Luke 2:19).

Chapter Eighteen

Women and Jesus

DO YOU THINK that because the central figure of Christianity is a male that you have to bow down to men? Or do you think that because he is a man you, as a woman, are left without a viable role model for spirituality?

Searching the accounts of Jesus' life one finds no restriction of gender — either in the person of Jesus himself nor in his dealings with women. Those women who might express themselves by saying they feel confined by Jesus' maleness must ask first if it is the Bible's accounts of Jesus or the accounts of the historical church that are troubling. Search the accounts of Jesus' life: You will find nothing that says women can't be priests or disciples or ministers. Still, no reader with an open mind will be satisfied with the patronizing attitude that says: Jesus treated women well, so what's the problem?

Why, some wonder, can't all men be like him — treating women as full and equal expressions of the spiritual Creator? The answer is not to romanticize Jesus and, by contrast, find the men in one's life a major disappointment.

To consider the enormity of the issue involved and to look toward where the answer dwells, ponder what Paul says: *When Christ, who is our life, shall appear, then shall ye also appear with him in glory* (Colossians 3:4).

Let's look at some scriptural examples of Jesus' encounters with women.

Jesus is to be circumcised. Luke's report puts us in the temple with Simeon, *waiting for the consolation of Israel; and the Holy Ghost was upon him* (Luke 2:25). And, as Luke hardly ever tells a story about a man without then telling about a woman, we see Anna, a prophetess.

She is of the tribe of Asher and she is a widow of great age (about eighty-four), and *she served God with fastings and prayers night and day. And she coming in that instant gave thanks likewise unto the Lord, and spake of him to all them that looked for redemption in Jerusalem* (Luke 2:36–38).

Luke records Jesus' visit to the temple at the age of twelve. *And all that heard him were astonished at his understanding and answers* (Luke 2:47). Upon Mary's discovery of him there, Jesus declares to her: *wist ye not that I must be about my Father's business? And they understood not the saying which he spake unto them . . . but his mother kept all these sayings in her heart* (Luke 2:49–51).

It is not until after Jesus is baptized by John the Baptist, not until after *the Holy Ghost descended in a bodily shape like a dove upon him, and a voice came from heaven, which said, Thou art my beloved Son; in thee I am well pleased* (Luke 3:22), that Luke says: *And Jesus himself began to be about thirty years of age, being (as was supposed) the son of Joseph* (Luke 3:23).

And after all this Luke begins a biological genealogy of Jesus. (Luke 3:23–38)

Women ministering

Luke says that the political, economic and social temptations that Jesus faces in the wilderness (4:1–16) preface his return to Galilee in the power of the Spirit — the same Spirit that moved upon the face of the *waters* in the first chapter of Genesis.

Preaching in his hometown synagogue, Jesus' reference to Elijah's healing of the widow woman makes people so angry that *when they heard this, all in the synagogue were filled with rage. They got up, drove him out of the town, and led him to the brow of the hill on which their town was built, so that they might hurl him off the cliff. But he passed through the midst of them and went on his way* (Luke 4:28–30 *NRSV*).

Holding up women and the afflicted — in this case the widow and the leprous King Naaman, who takes the advice of a captive servant woman (2 Kings, chapter 5) — as examples of when, where, why and how God comes to earth is not popular theology.

Nevertheless Luke's Gospel is a case study in human detail, gender balance and egalitarianism. Not only does he have the angel appear to Mary and not to Joseph; he is the only gospel author to give background information on Jesus' youth.

Luke's stories about men and women alternate. For example,

when Jesus leaves the synagogue and *passing through the midst of them went his way to a city in Galilee* (Luke 4:30), he first rebuked and *cast devils* out of a man (Luke 4:35) and then healed the mother-in-law of Simon (Peter) by rebuking a *great fever* (Luke 4:38). He then healed any and *all the sick* brought to him (Luke 4:40). You can see that the pattern here is man, then woman, then all, as an echo of the first chapter of Genesis.

After a feast given for Jesus in a *great house,* Luke records that he talked of the *children of the bridechamber and the bridegroom,* spoke of sewing while alluding to spiritual Creation, talked about *wine* — new and old (Luke 5:29–39). In the first half of chapter 7, he healed a man who is not physically present and then, as Elijah did, restored to a widow that which was lost by raising her son from the dead. And then again, he *heals many of their infirmities.*

A story that no woman who reads the Bible should miss is the story of the woman who — at an otherwise all-male dinner — washes Jesus' feet (Luke 7:36–50). The story exposes male sexism. It's a profound look at the who, what, when, where and why of women and men and the forgiveness of sin.

Jesus goes, by invitation, to a Pharisee's house.

> *And, behold, a woman in the city, which was a sinner, when she knew that Jesus sat at meat in the Pharisee's house, brought an alabaster box of ointment, And stood at his feet behind him weeping, and began to wash his feet with tears, and did wipe them with the hairs of her head, and kissed his feet, and anointed them with the ointment.* (Luke 7:37–38)

The Pharisee leaps to a conclusion, saying to himself that if Jesus were a prophet, he would know that the woman touching him was a sinner.

If you start thinking at this point in the story about the customs of Oriental religions, where monks and prophets are not to be touched by women, you will miss the point. This story is not about history as much as it is about how men view women through the lens of sexuality: *"Do you see this woman?* (Luke 7:44 *NIV*).

Look at the scene not from the perspective of the men, but of the woman. If you put yourself in the place of the woman, you will see that she knew what she was doing. Jesus knew what she was doing. And, as you read the story for yourself, it will be hard to miss that the other men at the dinner didn't.

Shifting the point of view from a male to a female perspective changes the way we think about the story. Hospitality is again the key. The woman, who was not invited, comes anyway. It is she, not the host, who recognizes Jesus as guest, and the woman, not the host, who washes his feet.

Water, a central biblical theme, is to be found here. It takes form in the tears of a woman. The woman, fulfilling the function of a priest, *anoints* Jesus' feet and washes them with her tears.

She loved much (Luke 7:47). Love is the story's refrain.

It is the woman's actions, not those of the Pharisee nor even those of Jesus, that set the standard. Later, at the Passover Last Supper, Jesus will follow the example of this woman and wash the disciples' feet.

Jesus says to the woman that her sins are forgiven. He is saying to her that she is doing the right thing, not the wrong thing. In Hebrew the word for sin means "to miss the mark." She is not missing the mark.

The woman is to experience the opposite of punishment — *go in peace* (Luke 7:50).

Although some have speculated that this woman is Mary Magdalene, in fact in the Bible she has no name. That she has no name underlines the timelessness of the story. The woman is unnamed not because she is unimportant but because with no name she is any of us, all of us. To insist that she is Mary Magdalene hides the essence of the story by localizing sin and forgiveness in a sexual context. And further, it's biblically incorrect as you will see when you find Mary Magdalene in other gospel accounts.

After this story, the disciples and Mary Magdalene and Joanna and Susanna and many other unnamed women go throughout the cities and towns with Jesus (Luke 8:1–3). The Bible says it is the women who minister to him and that the first story Jesus told on this trip with the women was about seed as the Word of God. We are again reminded of the woman and her seed and attacks on woman's seed.

In the face of the biblical evidence, it hardly seems possible that there is any argument about whether women can be *ministers*. Perhaps the hitch is that Luke reported that Peter's mother-in-law *ministered unto them* (Luke 4:39); some read this to mean that ministering means domestic duty. But Luke says that women *ministered unto him* (Jesus) *of their substance* (Luke 8:3). Biblical substance is something you ought to look deeply into here to probe the idea of both ministry and *substance.*

Blood

Luke's stories about healings are woven together in significant ways. This is made startlingly clear in his recounting of the healing of *a woman with an issue of blood twelve years* juxtaposed with the raising from the dead of a *twelve-year*-old girl (Luke 8:43–56). Implicit associations with menstruation and explicit statements calling both women *daughter* indicate Jesus' perception of these women as loved by the Father-Mother God.

By his actions Jesus makes clear that the curse on Eve does not apply to any other woman.

As Luke tells the story the notion that the Bible denies the body seems senseless. It is in the body that healing happens. Mark tells a story of a woman who suffered bleeding for years before she was healed by Jesus. *And straightway the fountain of her blood was dried up; and she felt in her body that she was healed of that plague* (Mark 5:29).

So much has been said, thought and done in the name of the Jesus of the Bible that the only sensible way to answer the questions at the start of this chapter is to read his biography and decide for yourself.

John says, at the end of his gospel:

Jesus did many other things as well. If every one of them were written down, I suppose that even the whole world would not have room for the books that would be written.

(John 21:25 *NIV*)

But what is written in the Bible is certainly the place to start.

Chapter Nineteen

Sisters

W HAT IF THE BIBLE SAID that wherever the gospel is preached it is what a woman did that will be remembered?

Martha and Mary are sisters. And they are unlike. The differences in their approaches to what is required by life may indicate two entirely separate schools of thought. If you have a sister — biological or spiritual — this dichotomy may sound familiar.

Luke 10:40 tells how *Martha was cumbered about much serving,* but the story, as told in chapters 11 and 12 of John, is a book in itself.

This familiar story is another easy place to practice reading the Bible critically. As you look at the story of the sisters, you will see that the first verse says that *a certain man was sick, named Lazarus of Bethany* (John 11:1) and that the town of Bethany is not the town of Lazarus but the town of Mary and her sister Martha.

The relationship of the women as sisters is mentioned, but it is only in the next verse we learn, parenthetically, that this certain man is their brother: (*It was that Mary which anointed the Lord with ointment, and wiped his feet with her hair, whose brother Lazarus was sick.*) (John 11:2)

This is a not a reference to the unnamed woman earlier in Luke — assumed to be Mary of Magdala — but a specific reference to this Mary of Bethany. She is one of several women who *anoint* Jesus. (Remember — the title *Christ* translates from the Greek as "anointed.")

Read on and you may think it seems strange that six verses are spent sorting out relationships when, after all, this is a story about the who, what, when, where and why of resurrection. Thus, this series of identifications and balancings takes on shades of meaning and varying hues.

Jesus waits two days after he hears that Lazarus is sick. He goes to

148

Judea and finds Lazarus, dead four days, and *many Jews comforting Martha and Mary* (John 11:19).

Martha rushes out upon Jesus' arrival; Mary waits to be called. Some women meet things head-on, questioning. Others wait to be called. Most women embrace both approaches at one time or another in their life.

> *"Lord," Martha said to Jesus, "if you had been here, my brother would not have died. But I know that even now God will give you whatever you ask."*
>
> *Jesus said to her, "Your brother will rise again."*
>
> *Martha answered. "I know he will rise again in the resurrection at the last day."* (John 11:21–24 *NIV*)

But Jesus challenges her theology with the then-radical, now-familiar:

> *"I am the resurrection and the life. He who believes in me will live, even though he dies; and whoever lives and believes in me will never die. Do you believe this?"*
>
> *"Yes, Lord," she told him, "I believe that you are the Christ, the Son of God, who was to come into the world."*
>
> (John 11:25–27 *NIV*)

Martha identifies Jesus as the Christ. And then she goes and calls her sister Mary and says that the Teacher is asking for her.

Mary gets up quickly and goes to Jesus, falling at his feet, repeating what Martha said, *"Lord, if you had been here, my brother would not have died . . . "* (John 11:21 *NIV*). She is weeping, but instead of raising a theological concept (as he did in response to Martha), Jesus is deeply moved in spirit. In fact, *Jesus wept* (John 11:35 *NIV*). He wants to know where the tomb is.

Moved once more, Jesus orders the stone rolled away from Lazarus' tomb. *Martha, the sister of him that was dead, saith unto him, Lord, by this time he stinketh: for he hath been dead four days.* (John 11:39)

"Did I not tell you that if you believed you would see the glory of God?" Jesus responds (John 11:40 *NIV*).

After Martha hears that, Jesus thanks God for hearing him always, and then, in a loud voice says, *Lazarus, come forth* (John 11:43), and, as Lazarus walks out of the tomb in graveclothes, to the crowd standing by, *Loose him, and let him go* (John 11:44).

Does this mean they should unwrap the graveclothes or does it also mean to let go of thinking of Lazarus as dead?

Then many of the Jews which came to Mary, and had seen the things which Jesus did, believed on him. (John 11:45)

It is not Lazarus, nor is it Martha to whom the Jews *who had seen come.* They come to Mary.

The news of Lazarus' resurrection gets back to the Pharisees. From that day forward they plan Jesus' death (John 11:53). Jesus, dwelling at the *right hand* of God, is nourished, until, with the full knowledge there is a warrant out for his arrest and that the crucifixion is near, he goes to Bethany for Passover.

There they made him a supper; and Martha served: but Lazarus was one of them that sat at the table with him. Then took Mary a pound of ointment of spikenard, very costly, and anointed the feet of Jesus, and wiped his feet with her hair: and the house was filled with the odour of the ointment. (John 12:2–3)

Mark tells a similar story. It takes place in Bethany, but there is no mention of Martha's serving. There is an elaboration of the anointing of oil on the head by a woman. After telling Judas to *"leave her alone . . . "* Jesus says, *"I tell you, wherever the good news is preached all over the world, what she has done will also be told in memory of her"* (Mark 14:3–9 *AT*).

Chapter Twenty

Ask and Receive

HOW DO YOU GET IN TOUCH WITH GOD? Prayer has long been an answer. Standing, sitting or kneeling? In a group or by yourself?

In early biblical narratives, before the establishment of any church or temple, people talked with God and angels as readily as we talk now with each other. Some simply converse with God; Hannah prays silently; others lift up their eyes. When you don't know what to do, then at least you can start by knowing what not to do. That's what the Bible does — alternating what not to do with what to do. All four gospel writers report Jesus' instruction on how to pray.

Jesus begins with what not to do:

Therefore when thou doest thine alms, do not sound a trumpet before thee, as the hypocrites do in the synagogues and in the streets, that they may have glory of men. Verily I say unto you, They have their reward.

But when thou doest alms, let not thy left hand know what thy right hand doeth: That thine alms may be in secret: and thy Father which seeth in secret himself shall reward thee openly.

(Matthew 6:2–4)

There is more of what not to do before one actually prays. Compare these statements of Jesus to your own idea of prayer and you'll undoubtedly find yourself in accord with the observations on hypocrites and those who play act at prayer.

"And then, when you pray, don't be like the play-actors. They love to stand and pray in the synagogues and at street-corners so that people may see them at it.

"But when you pray, go into your own room, shut the door and pray to your Father privately. Your Father who sees all private things will reward you.

151

"And when you pray don't rattle off long prayers like the pagans who think they will be heard because they use so many words. Don't be like them. For your Father knows your needs before you ask him." (Matthew 6:5–8 *Phillips*)

Don't be put off here by the use of *Father*. Its non-literal translation is "nourisher, protector, upholder, creator, preserver, guardian of spiritual beings." You will not be changing the spiritual sense of the following prayer if you are more comfortable substituting any or all of those words in place of *Father*.

Jesus' prayer

What is now called the Lord's Prayer reads:

After this manner therefore pray ye: Our Father which art in heaven, Hallowed be thy name. Thy kingdom come. Thy will be done in earth, as it is in heaven.

Give us this day our daily bread. And forgive us our debts, as we forgive our debtors. And lead us not into temptation, but deliver us from evil: For thine is the kingdom, and the power, and the glory, for ever. Amen. (Matthew 6:9–13)

Comparing Luke's record of the Lord's Prayer (Luke 11:2–4) with Matthew's is a simple way to see the differences in presentation of one central idea.

As you enter into your closet with this prayer, remember that there is so much to be pondered that you need to get only one thing a day. The Lord's Prayer, prayed over and over and over, unfolds and reveals itself.

Looking into Matthew's Gospel, you will find more of Jesus' commentary on alms, prayer, fasting and the body:

Therefore take no thought, saying, What shall we eat? or, What shall we drink? or, Wherewithal shall we be clothed? (For after all these things do the Gentiles seek:) for your heavenly Father knoweth that ye have need of all these things. But seek ye first the kingdom of God, and his righteousness; and all these things shall be added unto you. Take therefore no thought for the morrow: for the morrow shall take thought for the things of itself. Sufficient unto the day is the evil thereof.

(Matthew 6:31–34)

Test of prayer

There is no *Amen* in Luke's version of the Lord's Prayer. In his version, prayer is set in the context of friendship and family and healing. Look at the description of prayer in the verses that follow. At the reference to *three loaves,* make a note to look up the *woman,* the *leaven* and her *three measures of meal.* Not merely an example of how Jesus or Luke dotted their stories with references to the daily lives of women, the *three loaves* and *three measures of meal* are penetrating prophecy and theology. For those who want to journey on a profound path filled with intricate allusion, an inquiry into women's relation to *three measures, bread,* and *meal* is a terrific road to walk. You will remember to start with Sarah and the time she made *loaves* with *three measures* for the three men who came to visit unexpectedly. See how you might apply this following text to yourself:

> *And he said unto them, Which of you shall have a friend, and shall go unto him at midnight, and say unto him, Friend, lend me three loaves; for a friend of mine in his journey is come to me, and I have nothing to set before him? And he from within shall answer and say, Trouble me not: the door is now shut, and my children are with me in bed; I cannot rise and give thee.*
>
> *And I say unto you, Though he will not rise and give him, because he is his friend, yet because of his importunity he will rise and give him as many as he needeth.*
>
> *And I say unto you, Ask, and it shall be given you; seek, and ye shall find; knock, and it shall be opened unto you. For every one that asketh receiveth; and he that seeketh findeth; and to him that knocketh it shall be opened. If a son shall ask bread of any of you that is a father, will he give him a stone? Or if he ask a fish, will he for a fish give him a serpent? Or if he shall ask an egg, will he offer him a scorpion? If ye then, being evil, know how to give good gifts unto your children: how much more shall your heavenly Father give the Holy Spirit to them that ask him?*
> (Luke 11:5–13)

Matthew gives a specific, illustrative example of prayer.

A woman of Canaan, a foreigner and not a Jew, thinks she needs an intercessor when she goes to Jesus saying: *Have mercy on me,*

O Lord, thou son of David; my daughter is grievously vexed with a devil (Matthew 15:22). And Jesus doesn't answer her.

She does not go away moping or weeping.

She drives his disciples to distraction. She is so annoying that they go to Jesus and ask him to send her away.

He has still not answered the woman. His answer to the disciples is cryptic: *I am not sent but unto the lost sheep of the house of Israel* (Matthew 15:24).

The woman persists.

Then came she and worshipped him, saying, Lord, help me (Matthew 15:25). Jesus seems cruel and heartless when he answers and says, *It is not meet to take the children's bread, and to cast it to dogs* (Matthew 15:26).

Her answer is direct and to the point: *Truth, Lord: yet the dogs eat of the crumbs which fall from their masters' table* (Matthew 15:27).

Jesus replies, *O woman, great is thy faith: be it unto thee even as thou wilt. And her daughter was made whole from that very hour* (Matthew 15:28).

The woman with the confidence to speak truth to Jesus finds that it is in her power to get what she asks for. It takes persistence. She comes away not with a one-time healing but with the knowledge that her desire for her daughter's return to health is in itself a prayer.

It seems difficult for some to grasp that healing can happen in an instant or at a distance. But as the God of the spiritual Creation appears simultaneously throughout the universe and beyond, this is not outside the boundaries of the biblical text. Many report such healings today.

There is little question that the Bible is concerned about the care, feeding, wellness and understanding of the body. It is for the body that we primarily focus our need and want of healing. In the *light* of that need, perhaps we should examine more closely what our own bodies are and who controls them. Asking for this information, the Bible says, is the way to get it.

But what if healing doesn't come? Or what if we aren't getting what we really need to live? Again, this time in the Gospel of Luke, a woman's story suggests an answer:

And he spake a parable unto them to this end, that men ought always to pray, and not to faint; Saying, There was in a city a judge, which feared not God, neither regarded man: and there was a widow in that city; and she came unto him, saying, Avenge me of mine adversary. And he would not for a while: but afterward he said within himself, Though I fear not God, nor regard man; yet because this widow troubleth me, I will avenge her, lest by her continual coming she weary me.

(Luke 18:1–5)

The woman in this parable is the prototypical person who needs help in a world that devalues the woman alone. The Bible says that the widow, the woman alone — literally, metaphorically, physically or emotionally — is vindicated through her persistent need and prayer. Persistence and prayer may mean to figure out not only what you want but also what is standing in the way of getting what you want.

Challenge fear. Challenge the idea that you can't do something for yourself. Challenge every thought that says you don't deserve healing, or good, or all that makes up an abundant life. Don't give up, this parable says. God makes provision for you.

Beatitudes

A broken and a contrite heart. Meekness. Mourning (first introduced in the Bible when Abraham mourned for Sarah). There is much more in the Bible about provision than there is punishment, much more about love and humility than there is anger and pride.

Jesus looks back and echoes repeated biblical precepts (now referred to as the Beatitudes). Matthew describes the scene:

And his fame went throughout all Syria: and they brought unto him all sick people that were taken with divers diseases and torments, and those which were possessed with devils, and those which were lunatic, and those that had the palsy; and he healed them.

And there followed him great multitudes of people from Galilee, and from Decapolis, and from Jerusalem, and from Judea, and from beyond Jordan.

And seeing the multitudes, he went up into a mountain: and when he was set, his disciples came unto him:

And he opened his mouth, and taught them, saying,

Blessed are the poor in spirit: for theirs is the kingdom of heaven.

Blessed are they that mourn: for they shall be comforted.

Blessed are the meek: for they shall inherit the earth.

Blessed are they which do hunger and thirst after righteousness: for they shall be filled.

Blessed are the merciful: for they shall obtain mercy.

Blessed are the pure in heart: for they shall see God.

Blessed are the peacemakers: for they shall be called the children of God.

Blessed are they which are persecuted for righteousness' sake: for theirs is the kingdom of heaven.

Blessed are ye, when men shall revile you, and persecute you, and shall say all manner of evil against you falsely, for my sake. Rejoice, and be exceeding glad: for great is your reward in heaven: for so persecuted they the prophets which were before you. (Matthew 4:24–5:12)

The God of the Bible is not an angry man — though some see God this way. Something you might want to do to be comfortable with the God of the Bible and the lives of the people in its pages is to find the places in Hebrew Scripture where the Beatitudes appear. You might start by looking back to the reference to Moses as being *meek*. This is a starting point to seeing the Bible as the non-denominational story of the spiritual self.

Showing our children that God is not terrifying nor confined to national or denominational interpretations may unite us all.

The Golden Rule

If there is one thing almost universally agreed upon about the Bible, it is that it says, "Do unto others as you would have them do unto you."

Jesus sums it up this way in one translation:

Thou shalt love thy Lord thy God with all thy heart, and with all thy soul, and with all thy mind. This is the first and great commandment. And the second is like unto it, Thou shall love thy neighbour as thyself. On these two commandments hang all the law and prophets. (Matthew 22:37–40)

The mandate to *love thy neighbor* is called the Golden Rule. It's another fine place to share with children as you look with them for all the biblical precursors to Jesus' statement. Following this trail will acquaint you with the Law and the Prophets of the Hebrew Bible as well as many more of Jesus' thoughts. As you follow this trail, you need not feel that you will be trapped in the tangles of theology. Instead, you will travel through the wilderness with Moses and hear God's reminder that *ye were strangers in the land of Egypt* (Deuteronomy 10:19). And you will be in the way with Abigail, preparing meal and *bread* with Sarah, at the *well* with Rachel.

You will find yourself at the marriage feast at Cana where the *water* is changed to wine. You will drink of the inspiration that comes with seeing the women in the Bible not as chattel living in a bad time but as daughters of One God, Spirit, who is nourisher, protector, upholder, creator, preserver, guardian of spiritual beings.

Chapter Twenty-One

The Wedding

HAVE YOU EVER CHALLENGED THE ASSUMPTION that men were the only sources for the gospel accounts of Jesus' life? In some places, the accounts could have come only from women. And not surprisingly those accounts focus on relationships. Matthew, Mark and Luke say that Jesus began his ministry preaching in Galilee or a synagogue (Matthew 4:17, Mark 1:4, Luke 4:15). John begins his account of Jesus' ministry at a wedding.

All of John must be read to realize the full import of the nature and message of Jesus of Nazareth. Biblically, what has gone before and everything that is to come is alluded to by the ideas and words John uses in his gospel. But reading just the first chapter of John puts you back into the first chapter of Genesis and on into Revelation — particularly the last chapter.

Let's turn to the first words of John and to the first words of the entire Bible — *in the beginning.* As you read these passages in John, you see we are in *in the beginning* time with *all things made by God* and with *life as light* shining in the darkness (John 1:1–5).

John's Gospel says Elisabeth's son John the Baptist, sent from God, *was not that Light but was sent to bear witness of that Light* (John 1:8).

Looking at each verse of John reminds you of what has come before in the Bible. Let's follow just a few verses to see how this works.

Verse 29 says that the Baptist sees Jesus and calls him the *Lamb of God.* We remember Abraham and Isaac and the near sacrifice; we recall Abraham's statement: *"God himself will provide the lamb for the burnt offering...."* (Genesis 22:8 *NIV*).

The Baptist sees *the Spirit descending from heaven like a dove*

(John 1:32). We remember the *ruach Elohiym* and the *dove* that Noah sends out from the *ark* after the *flood* to see if it is time to come to *dry land* (Genesis 8:8).

The next day after his vision the Baptist sees Jesus pass by and says, *"There is God's lamb!"* (1:36 *AT*).

Two of the Baptist's disciples then follow Jesus. Jesus *turns* and asks them, *What seek ye? . . . Where dwellest thou?* they ask the Master (John 1:38).

God has asked Job, *Where is the way where light dwelleth?* (Job 38:19).

In John 1:39 Jesus says to the two disciples, *Come and see. They came and saw where he dwelt, and abode with him that day.*

Where did Jesus dwell? What did they see? What day? If you think that Jesus took them to some house, somewhere, in some town in the Middle East, and that they spent twenty-four hours there, then you might wonder why they would think and say, as they do, that they had *found the Messias, which is, being interpreted, the Christ* (John 1:41).

Andrew was one of the men who sees where the *Light dwells*. He goes and finds his brother Simon Peter.

He brings him to Jesus who, on seeing him, calls him *Simon the son of Jona* (John 1:42) — a reference to Jonah who spent time in the belly of the whale — and who, against his desires, preached to Nineveh and saved that city (Jonah 1:1–4:11).

Jesus then tells Simon that in the future *Thou shalt be called Cephas, which is by interpretation, A stone* (John 1:42). *Peter* and *Cephas* both carry the meaning "rock" or "stone."

The Baptist says, *God is able of these stones to raise up children to Abraham* (Luke 3:8).

Let's reflect a minute at where John's Gospel has taken us.

In the beginning, is the opening of John's chapter. This puts us into the unfolding days of spiritual Creation.

The first day mentioned in John's Gospel is *that day* that the disciples saw where Jesus dwelt (John 1:39) and where the *Spirit moved on the face of the waters* (Genesis 1:2).

The second day mentioned is the *day following,* John 1:43 and Genesis 1:3, where God said there is a firmament to divide the waters in two.

The third day of spiritual Creation pairs with *And the third day there was a marriage in Cana of Galilee* (John 2:1).

We are in the *third day* at the wedding — both in John's process of revealing the story and in the literal words. The story is set in the dimension of *the third day* of Genesis, where the *seed was in itself* (Genesis 1:12).

The Bridegroom

And the third day there was a marriage in Cana of Galilee; and the mother of Jesus was there: And both Jesus was called, and his disciples, to the marriage. And when they wanted wine, the mother of Jesus saith unto him, They have no wine. Jesus saith unto her, Woman, what have I to do with thee? mine hour is not yet come. His mother saith unto the servants, Whatsoever he saith unto you, do it. (John 2:1–5)

Let's assume Mary is the source for John's story.

Take yourself out of the everyday scene of the wedding — although there is certainly that element to John's story. Ponder instead the significance of the active participation of the mother of Jesus. We know her child was conceived spiritually. And we are at a ceremony uniting *male and female.*

Filling the *waterpots* with *water* (John 2:7) takes us again to the Spirit that moved on the face of the *waters.*

The changing of the *water* to wine has a spiritual connotation. *Water* is the essential element of Creation. *Wine* can refer to inspiration. This text can be read to mean that a more inspired sense of Creation — of union of *male and female* — is to take place at a traditional, very human wedding ceremony.

What John is talking about here is recreating Adam and Eve.

And when the governor of the feast tastes the *water* made wine, he calls the *bridegroom* (John 2:9).

Who is the bridegroom? John 3:29 has the Baptist comparing himself to the *friend* of the *bridegroom.* Do we simply assume that the *bridegroom* is the man being married that *third day* at Cana or are there other implications here? Each of the other twenty-two biblical references to *bridegroom* are messianic, metaphorical, proverbial or taken to be references to Jesus. You might look here at Isaiah 62:5 and see how the *bridegroom* rejoices over the *bride.*

Remember these points as we continue on our way to Revelation 21:2, where the Holy City is adorned as a bride for her husband.

The Christ

After the *good wine* at the wedding, Jesus and his whole family *went down to Capernaum,* and there weren't too many days before it was Passover and *Jesus went up to Jerusalem.* There he whips some money-changers out of the temple, speaks of the *temple of his body* and says that a man must be *born of water and of the Spirit* (John 2:12–3:5).

Women continue to hold center stage in the fourth chapter of John. The Baptist is still baptizing, and there is *water* everywhere; Jesus asks for a drink. The physical setting is, John says, at the site of Jacob's well. The background may be the well, but the conscious revelation of spiritual identity is the foreground.

A Samaritan woman comes to draw *water.*

Jesus says, *Give me to drink* (John 4:7).

Then saith the woman of Samaria unto him, How is it that thou, being a Jew, asketh drink of me, which am a woman of Samaria? for the Jews have no dealings with the Samaritans.
(John 4:9)

That Jesus sees beyond tribal or gender distinctions is often noted when describing the character of the man. But bearing in mind the significance that *water* plays in the rest of the Book, readers will draw deeper meaning from the exchange in John 4:10–26 between the woman and Jesus. Readers have noted that Martha and this woman of Samaria recognize the Christ as surely as Peter and Matthew do in the opening of his gospel.

There are references to a husband and husbands and to the woman's perception that Jesus is a prophet, and there is again evidence that time is neither past nor future but is the immediate present. In this exchange, Jesus says, *God is a Spirit: and they that worship him must worship him in spirit and in truth* (John 4:24).

There were only two people at the well — the unnamed woman of Samaria and Jesus. Who reported this encounter?

The woman leaves her waterpot and tells the men in the city to *Come, see a man, which told me all things that ever I did: is not this the Christ?* (4:29).

The men go out of the city and *came unto him* (John 4:30).

Come, see, she said, using the words Jesus used to the two disciples who had wanted to know where he *dwelt.* And they came.

There is no hesitation. The woman is believed, and the men do what she says to do.

The men listen to Jesus, and the woman hears from them that it is no longer because of her statement alone that they believe Jesus is the Christ. They tell her that they believe it: *not because of thy saying: for we have heard him ourselves, and know that this is indeed the Christ, the Saviour of the world* (John 4:42). Sad to say, some biblical accounts report that men don't believe women. Would it matter if they heard it from a man? Is it that one has to hear and see for oneself?

Mary, Mary, Mary

John's recounting of the infamous story of the woman taken in adultery (8:3–11) points clearly to the fact that sin is not necessarily the act but what you think about it. Jesus says, *He that is without sin among you, let him first cast a stone at her* (John 8:7). (You might want to look at verses 6 and 8, where Jesus stoops down to write on the ground and see if you think there is some connection to Adam's being made of the dust of the earth.)

Each man, convicted by his own conscience, stops throwing stones and one by one, the oldest first, they depart, leaving the woman alone with Jesus. There is no one left to accuse the woman of sin or to stone her. Only Jesus or the woman could have told the end of this story.

The woman in this story is unnamed. Again, she could be any or all of us. There is no reference in the story to confirm the popular misconception that the woman is Mary Magdalene. It is a puzzle how Mary Magdalene's name became associated with adultery or why she has been called a whore. Using a concordance to search the Scriptures for references to Mary of Magdala or Mary Magdalene, you will see for yourself how simple it is to clear up misconceptions — even those held for two thousand years.

The fact is that Mary Magdalene — either alone or with a handful of other women, depending on whether you read Matthew, Mark, Luke or John — reports the Resurrection of Jesus Christ.

But there can be no Resurrection without the crucifixion.

Jesus describes his crucifixion this way:

A woman when she is in travail hath sorrow, because her hour is come; but as soon as she is delivered of the child, she remem-

bereth no more the anguish, for joy that a man is born into the world. (John 16:21)

The particulars of the crucifixion are well known. There is a Passover Supper where Jesus breaks *bread* and *wine* (Matthew 26:17–29, Mark 14:12–25, Luke 22:7–20) and where Jesus washes his disciples' feet (John 13:1–20), as the unnamed woman washed his. Jesus prays in the garden of Gethsemene, enjoining his disciples to pray *that ye enter not into temptation* (Luke 22:40). Here Jesus prays to let the Father's will, *thy will*, not his, *be done* (Matthew 26:42). He is living the Lord's Prayer, moment by moment.

Judas betrays Jesus (Matthew 26:49). Jesus appears before the chief priests, elders and all the council; Peter, as foretold by Jesus, denies his Master. Jesus is brought before Pilate. Judas dies. Pilate questions Jesus. Jesus is sentenced to die, and they lead him away to crucify him (Matthew 26:57–27:31).

The account of the crucifixion as found in Matthew, chapter 27, ends with

And many women were there beholding afar off, which followed Jesus from Galilee, ministering unto him: among which was Mary Magdalene, and Mary the mother of James and Joses, and the mother of Zebedee's children (Matthew 27:55–56).

Mark's account is in Chapters 14 and 15 and says;

There were also women looking on afar off: among whom was Mary Magdalene, and Mary the mother of James the less and of Joses, and Salome; (who also, when he was in Galilee, followed him and ministered unto him;) and many other women which came up with him unto Jerusalem (Mark 15:40–41).

Luke says in chapter 23:

And as they led him away, they laid hold on one Simon, a Cyrenian, coming out of that country, and on him they laid the cross, that he might bear it after Jesus. And there followed him a great company of people, and of women, which also bewailed and lamented him. But Jesus turning unto them said, Daughters of Jerusalem, weep not for me, but weep for yourselves, and for your children. . . .

As Jesus gave up the ghost, . . . all the people that came together to that sight, beholding the things which were done,

smote their breasts, and returned. And all his acquaintance,
and the women that followed him from Galilee, stood afar off,
beholding these things. (Luke 23:26–28, 46, 48–49)

As you read the gospel accounts of the crucifixion, you can be
one of the women at the cross *beholding these things.* And, as you
put yourself there, you will witness John's account of the scene at
the cross:

Now there stood by the cross of Jesus his mother, and his
mother's sister, Mary the wife of Cleophas, and Mary Magda-
lene. When Jesus therefore saw his mother, and the disciple
standing by, whom he loved, he saith unto his mother, Woman,
behold thy son! Then saith he to the disciple, Behold thy mother!
And from that hour the disciple took her unto his own home. Af-
ter this, Jesus knowing that all things were now accomplished,
that the scripture might be fulfilled, saith, I thirst.

(John 19:25–28)

All four gospel writers say that on the *first day* of the week (the
day from Genesis when the Spirit of God moved on the face of the
waters), Mary Magdalene was at the tomb (Luke 24:1–10). Her story,
what she saw, heard, felt and did will lead you to the scene. Through
her experience the Bible reader is given a glimpse of the Resurrection. Through her experience you can follow for yourself how it
dawns on her what is going on and that she is witness, one who
carries the report to the apostles. And if she is the only witness, then
only she or Jesus could have reported the event.

Luke says that Mary Magdalene — along with Joanna and Mary,
the mother of James — reported to the *apostles* that they had seen
two angels who told them, *he . . . is risen* (Luke 24:5).

And, Luke says, *their words seemed to them as idle tales, and*
they believed them not (Luke 24:11).

Until the men see and hear for themselves they do not believe.

And beginning at Moses and all the prophets, he expounded
unto them in all the scriptures the things concerning himself (Luke
24:27).

Chapter Twenty-Two

Unity of Spirit

HAVE YOU EVER WONDERED just exactly what the Holy Ghost is? Mary, the mother of Jesus, in the first recorded meeting of what was to become the Christian church, met together with about 120 women and men who were disciples of her son (Acts, chapter 2). The people at this meeting included those who had seen Jesus and talked with him for *forty days* after the crucifixion.

The Books of Acts, Luke's account of what happened at this first organizational meeting of the Christian church, is, as is his gospel, addressed to Theophilus — *friend of God* (Acts 1:1). If you count yourself to be a friend of God, these accounts are addressed to you.

The Ascension, or disappearance of Jesus to human eyes, is reported in Acts 1:6–11. Jesus is taken up in a *cloud.* If you remember reading about Moses and the *cloud* and the Israelites not moving on their travels without the *cloud* going before them, then you see the interweaving of that message of Exodus with this report in Acts.

Crucifixion, Resurrection and Ascension are such extraordinary and powerful events that one wonders how there could be anything worth reporting after them. But just after the Ascension Luke reports that an issue at hand was to replace the traitor Judas with another disciple. This was done. There was prayer to know what the Lord wanted and then a vote by which Matthais was elected (Acts 1:24–26).

> *And there appeared unto them cloven tongues like as of fire, and it sat upon each of them.*
>
> *And they were all filled with the Holy Ghost, and began to speak with other tongues, as the Spirit gave them utterance.*
>
> (Acts 2:3–4)

The human form of Jesus is not seen but the presence of the *Holy Ghost,* the *Spirit,* comes to each woman and man in the *house* (Acts 2:1–5). This event is called the Day of Pentecost.

There is no disputation over theology. No separation of one group from another. The men don't gather in one part of the room and the women in another. They all speak their own languages, but when the word gets out, *every man heard them speak in his own language* (Acts 2:6).

Greeks, Egyptians, Persians all heard the speaking as if it were in their native tongue, but the people who were speaking in the Spirit were Galileans. Such was the effect of the Holy Ghost. It is the language of Spirit that communicates without regard to nationality. Jesus had promised this (John 15 and 16) and it happened.

There are eighty-nine biblical references to the *Holy Ghost.* Nearly half of them are in the Book of Acts. The first reference to *Holy Ghost* is in Matthew 1:18, where it is the Holy Ghost that fills Mary's womb with Jesus. The second-to-last reference is in the first letter of John: *the Father, the Word, and the Holy Ghost: and these three are one* (1 John 5:7).

One.

Read the following in the *light* of that One:

Have we not all one Father? hath not one God created us?
(Malachi 2:10)

In the beginning was the Word, and the Word was with God, and the Word was God. (John 1:1)

Hear, O Israel: The LORD our God is one LORD.
(Deuteronomy 6:4)

As you read the Bible, each and every time you see *Father, Word* or *Holy Ghost* remind yourself this is One. Non-denominational. Spiritual. And One.

The Spirit spreads

The church is organized economically so that all are one in financial resources. All throw in what they have and then the money and property are redistributed. And the focus moves away from the human form of Jesus, with the presence of the Holy Spirit available to all. In Acts, Luke reports healing after healing by the disciples as they lived in the afterglow of the Resurrection, Ascension and influx of the Holy Spirit.

But Peter put them all forth, and kneeled down, and prayed; and turning him to the body said, Tabitha, arise. And she opened her eyes: and when she saw Peter, she sat up. And he gave her his hand, and lifted her up, and when he had called the saints and widows, presented her alive. (Acts 9:40–41)

Note here that *saints and widows* are accorded equal weight.

One of the disciples, Philip, is transported instantly to and from a watering spot where he and an Ethiopian Jew read the Book of Isaiah in the *light* of the life of Jesus Christ (Acts 8:26–40).

There are martyrs stoned to death, there is great turmoil among Jews and Gentiles, and more people begin to believe the gospel of the eyewitnesses.

And at that time there was a great persecution against the church which was at Jerusalem. . . . As for Saul, he made havock of the church, entering into every house, and haling men and women committed them to prison. (Acts 8:1, 3)

Saul is on the rampage — *breathing out threatenings and slaughter against the disciples of the Lord* (Acts: 9:1). He is on his way to Syria to arrest more Christians, and he is converted by Jesus in a flash of *light* on the road to Damascus (Acts 9:3–9).

Chapter Twenty-Three

More Rough Places

WHAT ARE WE GOING TO DO ABOUT PAUL?

It is a very uncomfortable experience to hear Paul struggling, through the medium of church politics, to explain his converted vision of life in Christ. It is all the more uncomfortable when one knows that pastors and parishioners today are confronted with some of the same issues Paul confronted.

How should we respond to Paul's idea that women should keep *silence in the churches* (1 Corinthians 14:34)? Or that *the head of every man is Christ; and the head of the woman is the man; and the head of Christ is God* (1 Corinthians 11:3)?

Paul, the converted Pharisee, Saul of Tarsus, evangelist and eloquent and impassioned letter writer, missionary of the Christ, is condensed into and translated as saying a handful of things in his letters to specific churches and personal friends that have caused many women severe pain through the ages. Some women have a violent emotional reaction to even the mention of his name. Some love him. Others hate him. It has been suggested that to interpret Paul at all is to endorse sexism in religion. Others say to question him is heresy.

What he did to anger so many women today is to write letters. Letters from five men form the bulk of the New Testament. Paul, Peter, John, James and Jude wrote to friends while they traveled preaching and healing. If you are one of those people who write letters, you will appreciate that good ones are not easy to write and not often enough received.

Bearing in mind that Romans, Colossians, Timothy and Philemon are letters to people, their authors can be seen as men, not saints. Paul says he wrote only what his readers could understand.

Here is Paul in a translation of Romans 16:1–2 from *The Bible for Today's Family: Contemporary English Version:*

I have good things to say about Phoebe, who is a leader in the church at Cenchreae. Welcome her in a way that is proper for someone who has faith in the Lord and is one of God's own people. Help her any way you can. After all, she has proved to be a respected leader for many others, including me.

Paul goes on to send greetings to many women and men. In fact, all but seven verses out of the entire letter are personal messages to friends.

Paul's closing words to Timothy in another letter are: *When you come, bring the coat I left at Troas with Carpus. Don't forget to bring the scrolls, especially the ones made of leather* (2 Timothy 4:13 *CEV*).

Signing off, he says, *Give my greetings to Priscilla and Aquila and to the family of Onesiphorus. . . . Trophimus was sick when I left him at Miletus. Do your best to come before winter* (2 Timothy 4:19–21 *CEV*).

So much for the concerns of daily living. It is clear that Paul was a man before he was institutionalized as a saint. But merely recognizing the personal nature of some of Paul's concerns or his respect for women as his leaders cannot dismiss the agony that some women have encountered at specific statements made or supposedly made by him.

But each woman — if she is to find peace in the Bible — must carefully scrutinize Paul's statements in their context before accepting or rejecting them. Biblical context is the key here. And while it may be difficult to find peace in church, the Bible is another story.

An example: Paul seems to speak literally and in only one dimension when he says that women must wear coverings on their head in church while praying and prophesying. The issue of headcoverings — seemingly outdated to some but not to others — is discussed in the eleventh chapter of 1 Corinthians.

In Corinthians, Paul's words comment not on spiritual Creation but on the second creation of Adam and Eve. Today they may sound like sexual politics. But the biblical context is not male domination; it is instead prayer and prophecy.

But every woman that prayeth or prophesieth with her head uncovered dishonoureth her head, Paul's letter says (1 Corinthians 11:5). And he goes on to liken an uncovered woman's head to one that is shaven. In contrast, the unshaven head is a biblical sign of commitment and devotion to the Lord. Remember Hannah and her son, Samuel? Winding to an end Paul asks his readers to *Judge in yourselves* (1 Corinthians 11:13) because there is *no . . . custom* of contentiousness in the churches of God (1 Corinthians 11:16). Better to judge for yourself than get in an argument, he seems to be saying. To some, the rest of this letter of Paul seems concerned only with whether you've eaten or drunk before you come to church. To others, the letter is instruction in spiritually diagnosing one's body through Christ.

The range of readings of Paul is extreme.

There is the wonderful and familiar, *Though I speak with the tongues of men and of angels, and have not charity, I am become as sounding brass, or a tinkling cymbal* (1 Corinthians 13:1).

And then Paul cuts back to prophecy, which he emphasizes in 1 Corinthians 14: *Follow the way of love and eagerly desire spiritual gifts, especially the gift of prophecy. . . . He who speaks in a tongue edifies himself, but he who prophesies edifies the church* (1 Corinthians 14:1, 4 *NIV*).

Here and in the other places where Paul speaks about prophecy, women are included (1 Corinthians 14:24, 31). Paul says women prophesy and that prophesying edifies the church.

And then, just when you thought it was safe to go back into the waters:

> *women should remain silent in the churches. They are not allowed to speak, but must be in submission, as the Law says. If they want to inquire about something, they should ask their own husbands at home; for it is disgraceful for a woman to speak in the church.* (1 Corinthians 14:34–35 *NIV*)

It's thought by some scholars that this text is a "scriptural gloss." That means other people have altered Paul's words. In this view an anti-woman bias is the by-product of such revisionism. But that won't do for those who take each word of the Bible literally and who also believe all Scripture to be from God. Those readers may find consolation in the texts on prophecy and in the idea that God continually reveals Truth to each reader.

We can say that Paul had dazzling bursts of clarity when the mist thinned and we can say that there were times when he just didn't get it. We can say that was then and this is now. We can say that this or that text is inconsistent with Paul's other practices and professions on women and equality. We can say many things. What is certain is that Paul commented both on spiritual Creation and on Adam and Eve.

We all need more revelation. One might look at Paul outside the context of his times and in the context of the two Creation stories before arriving at a response to Paul and his message.

Look to Paul's own words:

> *I do not consider myself yet to have taken hold of it. But one thing I do: Forgetting what is behind and straining toward what is ahead, I press on toward the goal to win the prize for which God has called me heavenward in Christ Jesus.*
> (Philippians 3:13–14 *NIV*)

As to the question of whether or not women are to be silent in the churches, what are we to make of Peter's statement: *Knowing this first, that no prophecy of the scripture is of any private interpretation* (2 Peter 1:20)?

Here are some things concerning women and prophecy that readers might peruse to get them over the rough places:

> *And it shall come to pass in the last days, saith God, I will pour out of my Spirit upon all flesh: and your sons and your daughters shall prophesy, and your young men shall see visions, and your old men shall dream dreams: and on my servants and on my handmaidens I will pour out in those days of my Spirit; and they shall prophesy.* (Acts 2:17–18)

> *...and we entered into the house of Philip the evangelist, which was one of the seven; and abode with him. And the same man had four daughters, virgins, which did prophesy.*
> (Acts 21:8–9)

> *The words of king Lemuel, the prophecy that his mother taught him.* (Proverbs 31:1)

This last verse prefaces the poem long used in religious tradition to describe the ideal woman (Proverbs 31:10–31). It's a not-to-be-missed antidote to any feelings that womanhood is circumscribed.

Paul knew Scripture as few did and must have been familiar with this, one of the best-known passages. Because he was preaching a message of fulfillment of Scripture, and Proverbs puts no limitation

on women, Paul must have been in terrible conflict over what to say
to churches squabbling over sexual issues.

*Wives, submit yourself unto your own husbands, as unto the
Lord,* Paul says in a letter to the Ephesians (Ephesians 5:22).

Remember the last time you got in a car with your husband on
your way to an unknown destination. He didn't ask for directions.
You didn't know the way either. You suffered in silence; or you said,
"Yes, dear, whatever you say," and hoped it would all work out okay;
or you knew that God knows the way and leads you both to your
destination. There is nothing about the God of the first chapter of
Genesis that would have you wander in some urban or pastoral hell
at the mercy of a male ego.

Look at the whole of Ephesians chapters 5 and 6 and see how
everyone — including your husband — should act in the context
of the equality of relations that Paul discusses. This may all seem a
mystery at first blush, but look at what Paul says in Ephesians 5:32
about the *great mystery [of] Christ and the church* ("church," in
biblical Greek, is *ekklēsia:* like *Israel,* a feminine word.)

Paul sets his reflections on the relation of Christ and the church in
the context of two earlier biblical statements. One is that statement of
Adam in Genesis 2:24: *Therefore shall a man leave his father and his
mother, and shall cleave unto his wife: and they shall be one flesh.*

Paul is also talking about the spiritual union of *male and female*
(Genesis 1:27). It is here that you will want to return to the wedding
at Cana (John 2:1–11).

If chapters 5 and 6 of Paul's letter to the Ephesians are read in
the *light* of the first two chapters of Genesis and the first and second
chapters of John's Gospel, then any notion that Paul is discussing
literal marriage rules goes out the window. Paul himself says that
what he is talking about is a great *mystery concerning the church*
(Ephesians 5:32). Another word for *mystery* is *paradox* — a seeming
contradiction.

The importance of the relationship between what Paul says and
what is alluded to and spiritually described in the wedding at Cana
may seem obscure to those whose church, denomination or way of
worship doesn't include repeated references to Paul's statements as
the standard for marriage. But if you worship *where the husband
is head of the wife* is basic teaching, your husband may already be
loving you the way Christ loved the church and be *washing your feet*
as Jesus did the disciples'. And then again, he may not.

Peter too

There is little question that those who wrote the history of the church have interpreted some parts of letters that were written to one person or group at one time and pronounced that they should be the last word throughout eternity.

Yet there are inconsistencies, for example, between Paul and Peter. Peter says nobody with aspirations to an office in the church should drink wine, while Paul, in a letter to Timothy, suggests that Timothy drink some wine *for the stomach and other infirmities you have.*

Inconsistencies force the reader to acknowledge, at the very least, that even men deemed by other men to be saints were still men struggling with past history and contemporary mores. Each of us — and the men we know and love — are individuals at different states and stages of progress. But as the full and complete idea of who you are as God made you is already established, there is no reason to fear growth or change. Frustration with others who haven't reached their full growth disappears as you know who you are spiritually and prove it in your daily life. In any case, the Bible says sooner or later *the earth shall be filled with the knowledge of the glory of the LORD, as the waters cover the sea* (Habakkuk 2:14).

Paul also sees the impartial and universal nature of spiritual man. For example, he says, *There is neither Jew nor Greek, there is neither bond nor free, there is neither male or female: for ye are all one in Christ Jesus* (Galatians 3:28). Those women who do look into what Paul and Peter have to say about women will find that both these disciples comment on the first and second stories of Creation.

But if you are a glutton for punishment and sincerely want to tackle some rough places, take a look at Ephesians 5:25–33; 1 Corinthians 11:3–19; 1 Corinthians 14:34–40; 1 Timothy 2:9–15; and Titus 2:3–15. You'll see — as you read the surrounding verses — that they are at least sentimentally hopeful that both men and women will behave well on behalf of the whole community. But, while saving what is valuable about these words, do start to disentangle them from their literal reading if you want to get some rest and be taken on wings of an eagle to a place where you are *nourished for a time, and times, and half a time* (Revelation 12:14).

More mail; plain places

Though Paul waxes eloquent in so many of his New Testament letters, if you have only the time or inclination to read just a few letters, John's three letters should be among them. The first letter of John is a description of love. *God is love,* John says (1 John 4:8). We can't ask for more. John's first letter is also a description of the children of *light.* And a summary of the essentials of the consciousness of that Love and *Light.*

The second letter is written to a woman, *the elect lady and her children* (2 John 1:1). The historically minded may wonder who this woman was. As John has been called mystical, the mystically minded may wonder if this is one of those occasions of prophetic biblical times and deduce that the letter speaks not to one who got her mail at an address in a desert town but to, perhaps, the *woman* to come described later by John in Revelation.

Looking back and ahead

The last letter of the New Testament is Jude's. He reminds us of: Jesus Christ, God, Father, mercy, peace, love, faith, Lord, the people saved out of the land of Egypt, angels, Sodom and Gomorrah, Michael the archangel, Moses, Cain, Enoch, Adam, Holy Ghost, eternal life, compassion making a difference.

And before we get to the final conflict and resolution of the Bible, Jude says:

> *Now unto him that is able to keep you from falling, and to present you faultless before the presence of his glory with exceeding joy, to the only wise God our Saviour, be glory and majesty, dominion and power, both now and ever. Amen.*
>
> (Jude 1:24–25)

Chapter Twenty-Four

The Spirit
and the Bride

CAN YOU READ THE BOOK OF REVELATION as an exploration of the struggle for spiritual consciousness — your spiritual consciousness as a woman?

The Bible says it speaks to all people who ever hear it. The Book reveals itself. And, the Bible says, God is revealed to you as to the people whose experiences fill its pages.

The final book, Revelation, mirrors the struggle to accept individual spiritual revelation and to put that spiritual revelation into daily practice. It depicts in graphic imagery a war between *light* and dark.

The Revelation of Jesus Christ, which God gave unto him (Revelation 1:1) was given to John, in exile, on the Greek island of Patmos. John writes the words given to him directly by Jesus (Revelation 1:9–12). The revelation is addressed to all servants of God without limitation as to time or place. It is a book for everyone for all time.

In Revelation 22:18–19, there is a stern warning that the text is to stand as it is. As with the commandments, it may not be added to or subtracted from.

But to take Revelation too literally, to base one's theology on waiting for some future day, is to lose opportunities for spiritual growth here and now.

Summaries will not do justice to the force, power and message of Revelation. Given the nature of the Book of Revelation the best thing to do is read the Bible for yourself and see what Revelation says to you. The sketch that follows may help the reader with the overall structure of Revelation and a very few of the themes expressed there.

John, *in the Spirit*, hears *I am Alpha and Omega, the first and the last* (Revelation 1:10–11). This is taken to mean the first "man" and last "man" — that is, spiritual man with God, present at the last book of the Bible just as *in the beginning* (Genesis 1:1).

Those interested in biblical numerology and symbols have a field day with Revelation. Further, the Word melds its literary sense with its mathematical sense. Some readers have felt that some sort of codebook to Revelation is an absolute necessity, or they have relied on other people's interpretations.

For example, one vision that John sees is of a *lamb* with *seven horns* and *seven eyes* standing in the center of a colored *throne* (Revelation 5:6). What at first glance might seem a hideous monster is, in fact, a symbol of the complete strength and understanding of the Lord.

Jesus in his crucifixion is the *Lamb.* The *seventh day* is the day of completion of Creation. The *horn* is a symbol of strength, mentioned in Hannah's song (1 Samuel 2:1). Eyes represent sight and understanding. If we knew the Books of Ezekiel and Daniel, the Gospel of John, procedural ritual in the temple, the Hebrew theory of numbers and the uses of *horn* in previous Bible texts (as the people of John's time did) this revelation would not seem so obscure or difficult.

So many people study the Book of Revelation in so many ways that any summary seems presumptuous.

But to plunge ahead on our journey in very, very short form, the Book of Revelation consists of *seven* visions, which clearly allude to the *seven* days of the first Creation story. The *seven* visions are stated in a prologue and epilogue. The prologue is a message to seven churches and divides into seven parts. The seven messages to the churches, in chapters 2 and 3, address the qualities and characteristics of individual behavior, contrasting the best in human behavior with the worst. See if any of these touch on you and how you feel and act. (Remember as you read that *church* is a word in the feminine form.)

1. For example, in the first message, to the *church at Ephesus,* she has intelligently tested all things for herself and she has shown hard *work and patience* (Revelation 2:1–3). But she *left [her] first love,* either abandoning it or letting it weaken by not being as loving as she used to be (Revelation 2:4–5). Unless she changes her thinking immediately upon hearing this analysis of her behavior, she will be in trouble and bereft. But if she does return to her *first works,* she *gets the tree of life* that Adam and Eve missed (Revelation 2:7).

2. In the second message (Revelation 2:8–11), she claims that

she is poor when she is really rich. But if she can *remain faith-ful* and overcome misrepresentation of herself, she shall not miss *resurrection.*

3. Revelation 2:12–17: If she strives to overcome her struggles with idol worship and promiscuity, she will receive a new name, on a *white stone,* a name *which no man knoweth.*

4. Revelation 2:18–28: She is loving and faithful and has worked hard, but she allowed the *woman Jezebel* to teach and seduce. Who-ever follows *Jezebel* will be destroyed. But the victor over *Jezebel* gets all power and the *morning star.*

5. Revelation 3:1–6: Her work isn't perfect in the sight of God. She has got to *hold fast* and *repent* and *watch* more carefully or everything will be taken from her. The victor over these stumbling blocks is to be *clothed in white raiment* and to hear her *name spoken* in the presence of God.

6. Revelation 3:7–13: She has an *open door* in front of her that *no man can shut,* and she has used her talents to the full. Her task is to hold on to this; if she does, she is a *pillar in the temple of God ... in the city of ... God, ... new Jerusalem* (Revela-tion 3:12).

7. Revelation 3:14–22: She is *lukewarm* in her devotion and practice, and alternating between cold and hot. She has forgotten the poor and is very proud of herself and her position in the world, but she is loved anyway. She will be rebuked, but as rebuke and chastening are a sign of love, she shouldn't worry. She will be placed on a *throne of dominion in the lap of God.*

What follows in Revelation is either a continuation of the experi-ence of Jesus or the explication of a further vision of John about the experience of Jesus. There are varying schools of thought. As you read, or as you live some of these experiences, you will decide for yourself.

Revelation describes seven visions, which are the steps in the destruction of the darkness by the *light* as revealed *in the beginning.* They are elaborate, fantastic and grotesque. They refer, directly and symbolically, to other parts of the Bible.

1. Revelation 4 and 5: Everyone is happy because the *Lion of the tribe of Juda, the Root of David* (Revelation 5:5), has opened the *book* and demonstrated spiritual life. The truth about God is out.

2. Revelation 6: *The four horsemen* emerge from the first *four of seven seals,* coming to *wage war* with the idea of God. This vision

illustrates that there is no absolute safety anywhere in the world. It is the Spirit that gives life.

When the *seventh seal* is opened there is *silence for half an hour* (Revelation 8:1).

3. Revelation 8 and 9: The silence is broken by *seven trumpets*. One-third of everything dies, but not everything. We are reminded there is always so much more left to work with than that which was taken away.

A *book* is presented, as it is in Ezekiel 3:3, *sweet as honey in the mouth* but *bitter in the belly* (Revelation 10:9). The good news about God is out, but it doesn't settle very well. The female is coming into her rightful place and it causes upheaval. This turmoil **is** reflected in contemporary times with all its furor over women's roles and the rights of women.

The fourth vision appears only after a description of the resurrection of *two witnesses*.

4. Revelation 12–14: *And there appeared a great wonder in heaven; a woman clothed with the sun, and the moon under her feet, and upon her head a crown of twelve stars* (Revelation 12:1).

She is pregnant. . . . *and she being with child cried, travailing in birth, and pained to be delivered* (Revelation 12:2).

Menacing her is a *great red dragon* (Revelation 12:3), the snake from Eden magnified. The dragon is waiting to *devour* her child as soon as it is born.

> *And she brought forth a man child, who was to rule all nations with a rod of iron: and her child was caught up unto God, and to his throne.* (Revelation 12:5)

The woman fled into the *wilderness* (Revelation 12:6, 14), where her place was already *prepared by God,* and she is *nourished* there. Take note. There is a place already prepared for your protection. But you must go there — as Mary and Joseph took the infant Jesus to Egypt.

Then there is war and *Michael and his angels fought against the dragon* and the great *dragon was cast out, that old serpent, called the Devil, and Satan, which deceiveth the whole world; he was cast out into the earth.... When the dragon saw that he was cast to the earth he persecuted the woman* (Revelation 12:7–9, 13).

And again, the woman is saved.

She is *given two wings of a great eagle,* to fly into her *place* in the *wilderness, where she is nourished for a time, and times, and half a time, from the face of the serpent* (Revelation 12:14). Throughout the Bible, God makes provision. Women from Genesis to Revelation receive provision.

But the dragon tries to give authority to a terrible beast: *And that no [one] might buy or sell save he that had the mark, or the name of the beast, or the number of his name* (Revelation 13:17).

This number is 666 (Revelation 13:18). This is the number that three times tries to reach seven (representing completeness) and three times fails.

Chapter 14 is a contrast to chapter 13. John sees a *Lamb* standing on *Mount Zion* and 144,000 with him who have his Father's name on their foreheads. Only these 144,000 know the new song and *these are they which were not defiled with women: for they are virgins.* [. . . *They have] no guile* [and] *are without fault before the throne of God* (Revelation 14:1–5).

If one reads these verses literally, one might say that only celibate males are to be saved. But that interpretation would be at direct odds with the Holy Scripture that has gone before and is yet to come in Revelation. One might surmise the meaning here to be in the arena of purity — no intercourse or communication with the false Jezebel. This is surely a biblical passage to ponder for yourself. The implications of the passage have profound weight.

5. Revelation 15–18: The war gets worse. *Seven plagues* arrive, destroying any desire to worship the beast (Revelation 15:1). For the first and only time in the Bible the place called *Armageddon* is mentioned: *And he gathered them together into a place called in the Hebrew tongue Armageddon* (Revelation 16:16). The word means "mountains of Meggido."

In chapter 17 a woman appears upon a *scarlet beast*. She is the opposite of the woman with the *twelve stars on her crown*, who represents the Motherhood of God. The woman on the beast, on the other hand, is *MYSTERY, BABYLON THE GREAT, THE MOTHER OF HARLOTS AND ABOMINATIONS OF THE EARTH* (Revelation 17:5).

Why mystery? This section records how evil is fundamentally unknowable. Not the real thing, some say.

The woman *Babylon* is destroyed, and with her all endeavors that do not flow from God (Revelation 21–24).

6. Revelation 19–20: A rider appears on a *white horse,* followed

by the *armies of heaven*. Out of his mouth comes a *sharp sword* (Genesis 3:24 tells of a flaming sword that protected Eden). Everything that does not come from God is cast into the *lake of fire* (Revelation 20:15).

7. Revelation 21–22: The old heaven and earth are gone, replaced with new ones.

And the *new heaven and new earth* — the new consciousness of Life — is represented as a reuniting of *male and female* from Genesis 1:27. *Ruach Elohiym* has moved upon the waters of all consciousness, all history, all life, all men and women and, in male and female symbols of utmost purity, we read of the *holy city prepared as a bride adorned for her husband*.

Let's look at what John writes:

> *And I saw a new heaven and a new earth: for the first heaven and the first earth were passed away; and there was no more sea.*
>
> *And I John saw the holy city, new Jerusalem, coming down from God out of heaven, prepared as a bride adorned for her husband. And I heard a great voice out of heaven saying, Behold, the tabernacle of God is with men, and he will dwell with them, and they shall be his people, and God himself shall be with them, and be their God.*
>
> *And God shall wipe away all tears from their eyes; and there shall be no more death, neither sorrow, nor crying, neither shall there be any more pain: for the former things are passed away.* (Revelation 21:1–4)

There is to be no more crying, sorrow, death or pain, because all that was associated with the curse on Eve is gone (Revelation 22:3: *And there shall be no more curse*).

Behold, I make all things are new (Revelation 21:5). The visions are over, indicated by the repetition of *I am Alpha and Omega, the beginning and the end* (21:6; 22:13).

The heavenly city has no *need of the sun, neither of the moon* (Revelation 21:23) but is lit by the *glory* of God, as in Creation where there was *light* before the sun or moon.

The struggle is at an end. The destruction of the dark by the *Light* is complete. The consciousness of the children of *Light* is brought into focus in graphic imagery. The children of Israel, along with others who have followed God, have seen the *cloud* and the *glory,* fought the fight, dwelt among the heathen, gone repeatedly astray, dwelt with conscious awareness of the Law and the Prophets, sojourned with women and men who live, love, die, come to terms with their heritage and receive the Revelation.

Revelation 22 promises that anyone who has made it through the struggle to recognize the Power, Allness and Goodness of God, the Omnipresence and Omniscience of God, and managed to get past the huge deceptions, the terrible beasts and the surprising horrors that lie on the path to the holy city will be rewarded. The reward is the right to the *tree of life* and fulfills the promise of Genesis that the *waters bring forth life abundantly.*

At the beginning of the Bible we read of two creations. One records eternity and the other chronological time. After the accounts have been laid out, we see evidences of both kinds of time. Narratives give way periodically to reveal the eternal spiritual story, the face and voice, the understanding of the presence and power of God in the flesh and the daily affairs of women and men.

In Revelation the two stories have become one. We have reached Eden, but without the curse, without the serpent, without any deceit. The *male and female* are one again as they were *in the beginning.* The *Spirit* joins with the *bride* to say *Come* (Revelation 22:17). Anyone who will can take of the *water of life freely.*

Ruach Elohiym moves on the face of the *waters.*

Acknowledgments

Fᴀɪᴛʜ, ᴛʀᴜsᴛ, ɪɴᴛᴇʀᴇsᴛ, ᴘᴀᴛɪᴇɴᴄᴇ, ᴄʜᴀʀɪᴛʏ ᴀɴᴅ ʟᴏᴠᴇ in the most tangible ways came without measure from Karl Seitz, Michelle Zackheim, Charles Ramsberg, Florence Falk, Phyllis Montgomery, Bob Owens, Wilhelmina Harrell and C. O. McLaughlin.

My son Tom never failed to support and encourage me. Catherine G. S. Bonde, Torgils, Nicolas and Wilhelmina Bonde are owed a particular debt of gratitude.

My family, Martin, Hans, Elbjorg, Arnhild Hoel, Hallgard and Egil Torhaug in Norway, Helen Knudson, Marion Robman, Kay Studebaker and Bill, Mark and John, Sue Dosal and Frank, Elizabeth and Michael in Minnesota, Milnore Hall and M. O. Hoel in California and Jayne Buckingham, Brian and Mary Bundesen in Chicago and Russell Simon in New York are all a part of this work.

So too, Irene Webb, Liz Muther, Emily Ennis, Jane Birnbaum, Elizabeth Becker, Rev. Rebecca Anne Pugh Brown, E. W. Count, Mary Anne Dolan, Katherin Seitz, Reina Attias, John Mencken, my sister Karin Baltzell and my daughter Kristin. She has been with the work a long and patient time.

I never think of Psalm 133 without thinking of Philip Friedman. Not once has he failed to walk with me through the ebbing and flowing of the publishing process.

Bob Heller is what one wishes all editors were. Publishing with Crossroad makes writing worthwhile.

Victor Mather took me through a critical and early stage of this work. He will see his hand in this book.

Cathy Raphael took me through the last stage of the work. She will see her sincere clarity throughout the book.

There is simply no way I can thank them enough.

Ed Little and Merri-jim McLaughlin know what the travail cost because they have been with me every step of the way in this work for a decade and more.

But without Claudia Jessup there would be no book at all.

And, as hospitality to the woman within us is what this book is about, all thanks go to Claudia.

Appendix

The Women in the Bible

I N THE KING JAMES VERSION of the Bible the words *woman* or *women* appear 538 times. The words *man* or *men* appear 3,768 times. It's an error to use the numbers as any judge at all of the importance of women in the Bible because, from the spiritual Creation in Genesis 1:27 on, the word *man* means the "male and female" of God's creating as well as humankind in general. *Person* and *humankind* are contemporary words that indicate inclusiveness of woman and women, but *man* or *men,* as the Bible uses the word, may also be referring to *women.* The New Revised Standard Version reflects an inclusive approach.

The word *daughter* or *daughters* is mentioned more than 200 times in the Bible. The references to allegorical daughters are worth searching out. *Daughters of Jerusalem, daughter of Zion* and *daughter of Abraham,* carry special meanings and importance. The daughters of Zelophehad establish women's claim to inheritance (Numbers 26:33, 27:1, 36:11; Joshua 17:3).

God speaks of comforting like a mother, and mothers are central to the Bible. Not all are wonderful. Two types of mothers are represented in one story. There Solomon must decide who is the mother of one child (1 Kings 3:16–28).

Wife and *wives* is used biblically to refer to a woman married to a man and also to a nation and people in their relationship to God. Wives, like mothers, are not all wonderful.

Widows are the prototype of the religious or the person religion is to honor and treat the most highly. The standard of all religion is found in James 1:27: *Pure religion and undefiled before God and the Father is this, to visit the fatherless and widows in their affliction, and to keep himself unspotted from the world.* To grasp the full import of Bible messages look up and read all the accounts of *widow, widows.*

Below is a list of biblical women who are identified by their own names.

ABI/ABIJAH

ABIAH

ABIGAIL (prophetess; marries David)

ABIGAIL (sister of David)

ABIHIL (mother of Ahban and Molid)

ABIHIL (niece to David)

ABISHAG

ABITAL

ACHSAH

ADAH (second woman mentioned by name in the Bible)

ADAH/BASHEMATH (marries Esau)

AHINOAM (mother of Michel and Jonathan; Saul is her husband)

AHINOAM (marries David)

AHLAI

AHOLIBAMAH

ANAH

ANNA

APPHIA

ASENATH

ATARAH

ATHALIAH

AZUBAH (marries Caleb)

AZUBAH (queen: Asa her husband, Jehoshaphat her son)

BAARA

BASHEMATH

BASMATH

BATH-SHEBA

BERENICE

BILHAH

BITHIAH

CANDACE

CHLOE

CLAUDIA

COZBI

DAMARIS

DEBORAH (Rebekah's nurse)

DEBORAH (judge of Israel, prophetess)

DELILAH

DINAH

DORCAS/TABITHA

DRUSILLA

EGLAH

ELISABETH

ELISHEBA

EPHAH

EPHRATH

ESTHER/HADASSAH

EUNICE

EUODIAS

EVE

GOMER

HAGAR/AGAR

HAGGITH

HAMMOLEKETH

HAMUTAL

HANNAH

HAZELELPONI

HELAH

HEPHZIBAH

HERODIAS

HODESH

HOGLAH

HULDAH

HUSHIM

ISCAH
JAEL
JAH
JECHOLIH
JEDIDAH
JEHOADDAN
JEHOSHEBA
JEHUDI
JEMIMA
JERIOTH
JERUSHA
JEZEBEL
JOANNA
JOCHEBED
JUDITH
JULIA
KEREN-HAPPUCH
KETURAH
KEZIA
LEAH
LOIS
LYDIA
MAACHAH (daughter of Nahor)
MAACHAH (marries David, mother of Absalom, Tamar)
MAACHAH/MICHAIAH (queen, daughter-in-law of Solomon)
MAACHAH (concubine)
MAACHAH (daughter-in-law of Manasseh)
MAACHAH (ancestress of King Saul)
MAHALAH
MAHALATH (marries Esau)
MAHALATH (granddaughter of David)
MAHLAH
MARTHA
MARY (mother of Jesus)

MARY MAGDALENE
MARY OF BETHANY
MARY (mother of James and Joses)
MARY (mother of John Mark)
MATHRED
MEHETABEL
MERAB
MESHULLEMETH
MICHAL
MILCAH (marries Nahor)
MILCAH (daughter of Zelophehad)
MIRIAM
NAAMAH (daughter of Lamech)
NAAMAH (mother of King Rehoboam)
NAARAH
NAOMI
NEHUSHTA
NOADIAH
NOAH (daughter of Zelophehad)
ORPAH
PENINNAH
PERSIS
PHEBE
PRISCILLA
PUAH
RACHEL
RAHAB (heroine; along with Abraham, Isaac, Jacob, Joseph and Moses counted as faithful; possible mother of Boaz)
REUMAH
RHODA
RIZPAH

RUTH

SALOME (mother of James and
   John)

SAPPHIRA

SARAH/SARAI

SARAH (daughter of Asher)

SHELOMITH (marries an
   Egyptian, stoned to death for
   blasphemy)

SHELOMITH (daughter of
   Zerubbabel)

SHERAH

SHIMEATH

SHIMRITH/SHOMER

SHIPHRAH

SHUA

SUSANNA

SYNTYCH

TAHPENES

TAMAR/THAMAR (ancestor of
   David)

TAMAR (daughter of David, sister
   of Absalom)

TAMAR (daughter of Absalom)

TAPHATH

TARZAH

TIMNA

TRYPHENA

TRYPHOSA

VASHTI

ZEBUDAH

ZERESH

ZERUAH

ZERUIAH

ZIBIAH

ZILLAH

ZILPAH

ZIPPORAH

Bibliography

Bibles

The Bible: An American Translation. J. M. Powis Smith, editor, Old Testament; Edgar J. Goodspeed, editor, New Testament. The University of Chicago Press, 1935.

The Bible for Today's Family: Contemporary English Version. New Testament. Thomas Nelson Publishers, 1991.

The Good News Bible: The Bible in Today's English Version. American Bible Society, 1971, 1976.

Holy Bible: New Revised Standard Version. American Bible Society, 1989. Translating committee is made up of both men and women and inclusive language used as much as possible.

The New Jerusalem Bible. Doubleday, 1985. Notes and introduction 1990. Includes apocryphal books.

The New Testament in Modern English. J. B. Phillips. The Macmillan Company, 1958.

Tanakh — The Holy Scriptures: The New JPS Translation According to the Traditional Hebrew Text. The Jewish Publication Society, 1985.

Tyndale's Old Testament: Being the Pentateuch of 1530, Joshua to 2 Chronicles of 1537, and Jonah. Translated by William Tyndale in the modern spelling edition and with an introduction by David Daniell. Yale University Press, 1992. Forms the basis of the King James Version; translated by Tyndale directly from the Hebrew in 1530, five years before he was executed for his zeal and translation efforts and three decades before verses were installed by printer Robert Etienne. Fresh and new.

Study Aids

Gesenius, H. W. F. *Gesenius' Hebrew-Chaldee Lexicon to the Old Testament*. Grand Rapids: Baker Book House Company, 1979.

Strong, James, S.T.D., LL.D. *Strong's Exhaustive Concordance*. Grand Rapids: Baker Book House Company, reprinted 1987. A must for the King James Version of the Bible.

Thayer, Joseph H. *Thayer's Greek-English Lexicon of the New Testament*. Grand Rapids: Baker Book House Company 1977.

Selected Works

Alter, Robert. *The Art of Biblical Narrative*. New York: Basic Books, 1981.

Auerbach, Eric. *Mimesis: The Representation of Reality in Western Literature*. Princeton, N.J.: Princeton University Press, 1953.

Austin, Mary. *Christ in Italy: Being the Adventures of a Maverick among Masterpieces*. New York: Duffield and Company, 1912.

Bal, Mieke. *Death and Dissymmetry: The Politics of Coherence in the Book of Judges*. Chicago and London: University of Chicago Press, 1988.

Bernard, Bruce. *The Bible and Its Painters*. London: Macdonald and Co., 1983.

Buber, Martin. *On the Bible: Eighteen Studies*. New York: Schocken Books, 1968.

Carmody, Denise Lardner. *Biblical Woman: Contemporary Reflections on Spiritual Texts*. New York: Crossroad, 1988.

Chase, Mary Ellen. *The Bible and the Common Reader*. New York: Macmillan, 1944.

Chute, Marchette. *The End of the Search*. Harrington Park, N.J.: Robert H. Sommer, 1947.

———. *The Search for God*. Harrington Park, N.J.: Robert H. Sommer, 1969.

Corn, Alfred, ed. *Contemporary Writers on the New Testament*. New York: Viking, 1990.

Croatto, J. Severino. *Biblical Hermeneutics*. Translated by Robert R. Barr. Maryknoll, N.Y.: Orbis Books, 1984.

Curzon, David. *The Gospels in Our Image: An Anthology of Twentieth-Century Poetry Based on Biblical Texts*. Forthcoming.

Davies, Paul. *God and the New Physics*. New York: Simon and Schuster, 1983.

Deen, Edith. *All the Women of the Bible*. New York: Harper and Row, 1955.

Eddy, Mary Baker. *Science and Health with Key to the Scriptures*. Boston: Christian Science Publishing Society, 1875; renewed 1934.

Enslin, Morton Scott. *The Literature of the Christian Movement*. New York: Harper Torchbooks, 1938.

Frye, Northrop. *The Great Code: The Bible in Literature*. New York: Harcourt Brace Jovanovich, 1981.

Frymer-Kensky, Tikva. *In the Wake of the Goddesses: Women, Culture, and the Biblical Transformation of Pagan Myth*. New York: Free Press, 1992.

Gates, Henry Lewis, Jr., gen. ed. *The Schomburg Library of Nineteenth-Century Black Women Writers: Spiritual Narratives*. New York: Oxford University Press, 1988.

Girard, Rene. *Violence and the Sacred*. Translated by Patrick Gregory. Baltimore: Johns Hopkins University Press, 1977.

———. *The Scapegoat*. Translated by Yvonne Freccero. Baltimore: Johns Hopkins University Press, 1986.

Goldman, Rabbi Alex J. *Power of the Bible: The Eternal Books Retold*. New York: Fountainhead, 1974.

Gottschalk, Stephen. "Theodicy after Auschwitz and the Reality of God." *Union Seminary Quarterly Review* 41 (1987): 77–91.

Green, Arthur, ed. *Jewish Spirituality: From the Bible through the Middle Ages*. New York: Crossroad, 1987.

Grissen Lillian Y., ed. *For Such a Time as This . . . Twenty-Six Women of Vision and Faith Tell Their Stories*. Grand Rapids: Wm. B. Eerdmans, 1991.

Grosz, Elizabeth. *Sexual Subversions*. Sydney: Allen and Unwin, 1989.

Hartill, Rosemary. *Writers Revealed*. New York: Peter Bedrick Books, 1989.

Heilbrun, Carolyn G. *Writing a Woman's Life*. New York: Ballantine, 1988.

Herr, Ethel L. *Chosen Women of the Bible*. Chicago: Moody Press, 1976.

James, William. *The Varieties of Religious Experience*. New York: Macmillan, 1961.

Josipivici, Gabriel. *The Book of God: A Response to the Bible*. New Haven and London: Yale University Press, 1988.

Kermode, Frank. *The Genesis of Secrecy: On the Interpretation of Narrative*. Cambridge, Mass., and London: Harvard University Press, 1979.

Knox, Ronald A. *Commentary on the Gospels*. New York: Sheed and Ward, 1952.

Kolbenschlag, Madonna, ed. *Women in the Church*. Washington, D.C.: Pastoral Press, 1987.

Luther, Martin. *Martin Luther: Selections from His Writings*. John Dillenberger, ed. New York: Anchor Books, 1961.

Mann, Thomas. *Joseph and His Brothers*. Translated by H. T. Lowe-Porter. 15th ed. New York: Alfred A. Knopf, 1988.

May, Melanie A. *Women and Church: The Challenge of Ecumenical Solidarity in an Age of Alienation*. Grand Rapids: Wm. B. Eerdmans, and New York: Friendship Press, 1991.

Mollenkott, Virginia Ramey. *Women of Faith in Dialogue*. New York: Crossroad, 1987.

Mozeson, Isaac E. *The Word: The Dictionary That Reveals the Hebrew Source of English*. New York: Shapolsky Publishers, 1989.

Newman, Barbara. *Sister of Wisdom, St. Hildegard's Theology of the Feminine*. Berkeley and Los Angeles: University of California Press, 1987.

Plaskow, Judith. *Standing Again at Sinai: Judaism from a Feminist Perspective*. San Francisco: Harper and Row, 1990.

Preminger, Alex, and Edward L. Greenstein, compilers and editors. *The Hebrew Bible in Literary Criticism*. New York: Ungar, 1986.

Provian, Ian. *The New Century Bible Commentary: Lamentations*. Grand Rapids: Wm. B. Eerdmans, 1991.

Renckens, H., S.J. *Israel's Concept of the Beginning: The Theology of Genesis 1–111*. New York: Herder and Herder, 1964.

Rose, Jacqueline. *Sexuality in the Field of Vision*. London: Verso, 1986.

Rosenberg, David, ed. *Congregation: Contemporary Writers Read the Jewish Bible*. San Diego, New York, London: Harcourt Brace Jovanovich, 1987.

Schwartz, Regina, ed. *The Book and the Text: The Bible and Literary Theory*. Cambridge, Mass.: Basil Blackwell, 1990.

Shotwell, Berenice Myers. *Getting Better Acquainted with Your Bible*. Kennebunkport, Maine: Shadwold Press, 1972.

Steinsaltz, Adin. *Biblical Images: Men and Women of the Book*. Trans. Yehuda Hanegbi and Yehudit Keshe. New York: Basic Books, 1984.

Stowe, Harriet Beecher. *Women in Sacred History: A Celebration of Women in the Bible*. New York, 1873; new edition, New York: Portland House, 1990.

Trible, Phyllis. *God and the Rhetoric of Sexuality*. Minneapolis: Augsburg Fortress, 1978.

————. *Texts of Terror: Literary-Feminist Readings of Biblical Narratives*. Minneapolis: Augsburg Fortress, 1984.

Weidman, Judith L., ed. *Christian Feminism: Visions of a New Humanity*. San Francisco: Harper and Row, 1984.

Zinsser, William, ed. *Spiritual Quests: The Art and Craft of Religious Writing*. Boston: Houghton Mifflin, 1988.

Zuntz, G. *Opuscula Selecta: Classica Hellenistica Christiana*. Manchester: Manchester University Press, 1972.